bomb pops®,
blow dryers,
& butterfly kisses

bomb pops®,
blow dryers,
& butterfly kisses

a journey of healing.

a story of hope.

Angelia Waite, M.Div.

First Edition

ISBN: 978-0-9860988-0-2

Managing editor: Alice Sullivan, alicesullivan.com
Cover Designer: Kristen Vasgaard Ingebretson, PenMeetPaper.com
Typesetter: Mandi Cofer, thetinytypesetter.com

Connect with us at AngeliaWaite.org

endorsements

Angelia, you have given a great gift to many with your highly human story, *Bomb Pops®, Blow Dryers, & Butterfly Kisses*. There is a tender, grace-attending insight into the hope and healing God's Word and presence bring to those who mourn.

—*Jack W. Hayford, D.D., Founder-Chancellor, The King's University*

The powerful impact of Angelia Waite's book, *Bomb Pops®, Blow Dryers, & Butterfly Kisses* is stunning in its depth. For anyone who has experienced tragedy or sudden loss, or for anyone who desires to minister life where death has taken its toll, this book will help transform what seems hopeless into radical hope!

With vision and intentionality, Angelia communicates how the Lord has demonstrated His presence through the severity of intense suffering and brought a fresh perspective of hope in the face of trials. She states in a quote from the book, "I am amazed at the tools God will use to minister to His children when they are suffering through the blows of this fallen world. He knows exactly what will penetrate each of our hearts to bring about healing, and He is faithful to provide it."

I highly endorse this resource and believe that the Holy Spirit will profoundly minister to all who read this inspired work.

—*Glenn C. Burris, Jr., D.D. President, The Foursquare Church*

Trials, tribulations, and tragedies have been intertwined throughout history. Every life and every person who has ever lived has experienced the pain of loss, heartache, and disappointment, some in depths unfathomable. But with God, "Beauty from Ashes" is not a cliché, but a "LifeSong!"

We have personally witnessed *His* remarkable story unfold in the lives of the Waite family. From the rubble of brokenness to the waves of healing to the crescendo of restoration, His faithfulness has rang true! Our journey with Him is holy—and being invited into someone's intimate walk, battles, and victories, is something that never should be taken lightly.

We are blessed to be their friends, we count it a privilege to have been a part of this story, and we consider it an honor to highly recommend the pages herein.

—*Rusty and Leisa Nelson, Co-Lead Pastors,*
The Rock Family Worship Center, Huntsville, Alabama

It is with the greatest pleasure that I recommend this tremendous book! I have known Angelia Waite since our seminary days as my classmate, friend, and mentor. Having gone through cathartic life experiences and intensely vigorous training with the Scriptures, she speaks with authority on this subject of grief and loss. With passionate compassion she imparts heart-transforming Truths to those who are in desolate and dark places. Get ready to know the Lord more intimately as you travel together with this amazing author from the depth of despair to the glorious fellowship with our Risen Lord.

—*Lily Yang, M.D., FACOG, M.Div.*
LSU-S Assistant Professor of Ob/Gyn, Bible Teacher,
Trinity Christian Center at Forest Hills, LA

Bomb Pops®, Blow Dryers, & Butterfly Kisses is an amazing book for anyone seeking to understand how to navigate the hurt and pain experienced due to the tragic loss of a loved one. Angelia very articulately addresses the "how to's" in a way that is clear, concise, and God-centered. She not only shares the journey of loss, confusion, and ultimate healing that she and her family walked out, she also allows the reader to peek into the deep, dark regions of hurt that ensued after the passing of little Ramsey.

For those looking to understand how to help someone else through such pain, Angelia writes, "Love without words is best. No instruction needed, just embrace, weep alongside, and pray without ceasing."

Jesus is the same yesterday, today, and forever, and the hope offered in this book is this: the same God who showed up time and time again to help this grieving mother through her times of pain, awaits the heartfelt cry of all seeking His peace in the midst of tragedy.

—*Huey L. Hudson, Lead Pastor, Restoration*
Foursquare Church, Madison, Alabama

Having walked the grief journey with my husband's tragic death, I have a deep appreciation for the many-layered process of losing a loved one. Angelia's candor in both her testimony and her interactions with God lay a solid foundation, while her theological perspectives and practical insights beautifully blend to give the reader a complete "toolbox" for a complete process.

—*Rebecca Hayford Bauer, Author,* Life After Grief

Christ's followers are urged to "weep with those who weep" (Rom. 12:15), but we learn from Angelia Waite's experience that glib, careless, or academic responses to a grieving person only serve to increase their pain, rather than alleviate it.

This book proves that "people don't care how much you *know* until they know how much you *care*." One of the encouraging truths we get from Angelia and her husband, Jay, is that a marriage can be strengthened by the way a husband and wife together respond to the heartbreaking death of a child.

If you respond to this book as I did, you may find yourself "weeping your way" through it.

—*Harold E. Helms, Th.D, D.D. Former President,*
The Foursquare Church, Former Pastor, Angelus Temple

A.W. Tozer noted that whom God uses greatly, he wounds deeply. If this is true, then God will use Angelia Waite and her story in amazing ways. As I read it, I laughed, I cried, I was angry, and I found healing. This book exposes the compassion of God in the most isolated fringes of real pain. Angelia draws the reader into her pain in order that people might discover the amazing power of Christian assurance. Through it, the reader can realize the true context for suffering; it is not a destructive power, rather a pathway to hope.

—*John McKendricks, Executive Director,*
Multnomah University: Reno-Tahoe

contents

dedication

This book is in honor of Jacob "Ramsey" Waite. Our lives are better because he touched them. We love deeper, live louder, and dream bigger because of the impact that he left us. Until we see you again . . .

It is dedicated to all those hungry tummies, tearful eyes, and broken lives of little ones that will be touched as a result of this project. May the millions be given hope through it.

To my precious sons, Benjamin and Chandler: I couldn't have done it without you, nor would I have wanted to. I am forever grateful for the pushes, the shoves, and the constant reminders that this project was a necessity, and that healing for many was just on the horizon. Thank you for believing with me.

To the love of my life, Jay: Without your constant words of encouragement, your willingness to listen into the wee hours of the night, and your continuous love for me, I could not have penned the most difficult moment of our lives. You believed in me when I could not believe in myself. I love you with all my heart!

Thank you to Alice Sullivan, my editor. I never want to do a book project without you!

Without You: Father, Son, and Holy Spirit, I would not have survived to pen this book. May You receive all the glory from it!

preface

Proceeds from this project will fund Ramsey's Rescue orphanages in Ramsey's honor. Please join us as we prayerfully consider each location.

If you are finding yourself desperate for answers, I pray that this book brings peace to your heart. Whether you have buried a child; had dreams and hopes stolen; experienced a failed marriage, the foreclosure of a home, a debilitating illness, or any other type of devastating loss, I pray that you find answers in this book and that they bring back peace and hope.

Never give up.
Never give in.
Keep pushing.
You win!

In His arms,
Angelia

introduction

This is Ramsey's story and our healing journey. It only seems fitting that the introduction be his. So allow me to introduce you to Jacob Ramsey Waite.

———

He always carried a sword. He played dress up. He loved to wear hats. He had a smile that was often chocolate-lined. He picked flowers for me out of the flowerbeds. He played catch with his big brother, Benjamin. He jumped on the trampoline with his brother, Chandler. He carried the cat across his little arms and back into the house for safety. He gave butterfly kisses. He chased birds. He stopped long enough to smell the blooming roses and especially the yellow ones . . . his favorites.

It was a Wednesday afternoon and Jay and I were waiting in the preschool pickup line for Ramsey. This day was no different from any other Wednesday over the previous two years. Each time we picked him up he would share a brand-new experience. Perhaps he would give us every detail of how he had fished all day and how the toy whale bumped up against his boat, or maybe he would describe the train he saw as the class went for a "buggy ride" in the center of town. We were never sure what the new experience would be, but we were certain that each time we picked him up it would be as if he had not seen us in a week! There was always a flurry of giggling and hugging and butterfly kisses before we would ever leave the parking lot.

On this particular day as the teacher opened the car door to place Ramsey in his car seat, I immediately asked if he had had a good day and he was all smiles. She looked at us with a grin and said, "Ramsey doesn't put up with anything." What? I couldn't imagine what she meant. She explained to us that Ramsey had been in time-out that day; they called it "sitting with Miss Sue." That was a surprise to us. Apparently "sitting with Miss Sue" was their way of reprimanding the children rather than a one-on-one time of nurturing as we had previously thought. Ramsey would often tell us that he got to sit outside with Miss Sue, and we always thought it was sweet. Now suddenly it was obvious that having two older brothers to teach him the ropes was molding him into a little rough-and-tumble boy who spoke up for himself.

Attending Mom's Morning Out at the local Methodist Church was one of Ramsey's favorite events. He called it "playing with the kids." He would ask, "Is today the day we play with the kids?" He had many friends there but his favorite was Taylor; they were inseparable and they did everything together. Ramsey came home often speaking of the fun times they had.

During dinner one night, he told us about his lunchtime

that day at school and started laughing hysterically when he said he ate Taylor's "deet dawg." We had packed Ramsey's lunch that day as usual and couldn't understand why he would be eating Taylor's *hot dog*. I asked if Taylor brought one for him or if he and Taylor swapped lunches. He laughed and laughed while explaining that when Taylor got up from the table for a bathroom break, Ramsey ate his hot dog. Yes, there were tears and gnashing of teeth over that "deet dawg." And it was another day that Ramsey would get to spend with Miss Sue on the playground.

Ramsey was also a charmer. My husband's elderly Aunt May was in a local nursing home and Ramsey and I would visit May weekly. She just lit up whenever I brought him over for a visit. Every week he toddled through the door and climbed into her chair. They would sit together giggling as he swept her soft cheeks with his long eyelashes. Oh, how butterfly kisses would bring such joy!

One day as I picked him up from school I told him we were going to visit Aunt May. He kept saying, "May, not Aunt May!" I tried to correct him all the way over to the nursing home but he continued saying, "May, not Aunt May!"

When we went into her room, he immediately greeted her as "Aunt May." I couldn't make any connection with the constant correction that he was giving me, but it continued over the next several weeks every time Aunt May's name was mentioned.

A month later, I was delivering cupcakes to his classroom for a celebration. As I walked into the room, I saw this tiny

little girl riding on a car alongside Ramsey. They were giggling and racing and crashing into each other. The laughter of
those two filled the room, and other children were standing
around watching the two of them. It was so precious.

When Ramsey realized I was in the room, he jumped
off his car and came running over to me. He placed his
head between my knees with his arms wrapped around my
legs—one of my favorite kinds of hugs. The tiny little girl
was observing from afar, so I walked over to her to introduce
myself. She looked at me with the sweetest smile when I
asked her name. She replied quietly, "Mae." And Ramsey
screamed, "*Mae*, not Aunt May." Aha!

As a mom of three sons, I have found all sorts of unusual
items in the pockets of their clothing just prior to laundry:
rocks, marbles, rubber bands, racecars, action figures, crick-
ets, nuts and bolts, pieces of wood, and, of course, pieces of
chewed gum mixed with melted chocolate. One particular
evening as I was undressing Ramsey for his bath, he busily
stuck his hands in his pockets to empty them instead of waiting for me to do it. This was a first—and it was a real surprise!

He loved climbing the magnolia on our front lawn
because it had very low limbs. This was one of his favorite
things to do, and I loved sitting in the breezeway reading so
I could watch him playing in and around the tree. Perhaps
the climbing caused him to feel powerful as he made his way
up the branches. He could sit on the second branch and look
below at the cat watching him. He loved knowing that she
was unable to reach him.

That night as he frantically dug into his pockets, he pulled out three bird eggs! He had not told me he'd found a bird's nest, and I never saw him take the eggs. Earlier that day, I had noticed him sitting very quietly on a branch, and as I looked over at him several times he gave me the sweetest, impish grin. That should have been my indication. But looking at the eggs, I was horrified.

I explained to him that since he had taken them from their nest, their mommy might not take care of them. Ramsey burst into tears. I tried to comfort him, but he was definitely preoccupied during bath time.

Now dry and clothed, he looked at me with those big brown eyes and said, "Mommy, I prayed and Jesus told me to put them back." Such a sweet boy. Okay, then put them back we will.

I allowed him to climb those two limbs. Then I handed him the eggs and he gently placed them back in the nest. We prayed over them that night, and that was enough for him— all guilt was gone. We never saw if those eggs hatched, but as best as I know, he lost interest in snatching eggs from their nests.

On another occasion, one chilly winter morning, Ramsey and I stopped in to visit my husband at his veterinary office. We were at the stage of attempting to replace Ramsey's bottle with a sippy cup, and he was a bit grumpy; but we continually handed him the cup or at least something to hold to take his mind off the bottle.

I sat down at the receptionist's desk because there was

no one in the waiting room. When the telephone rang while the receptionist was filling a prescription, I answered the phone, took the message, and then hung up. I looked down just in time to see a flood of milk pouring from a bottle all down the front of Ramsey's shirt. I quickly grabbed the bottle because I thought he had bitten the tip off the nipple. *But wait—he didn't have a bottle with him when we came in.*

The bottle belonged to an orphaned baby deer that was being nursed by my husband's staff. Ramsey was drinking from her bottle! I started screaming because all I could think of was all the germs he had just ingested. Everyone came running, and when they saw what Ramsey had done, they broke out in hysterical laughter—not a dry eye in the place. Ramsey was laughing so hard too. It was one of those moments you surely cherish . . . afterwards.

I am convinced that there was never a little guy more loving, caring, and giving than Ramsey. It was almost as if he knew his time was going to be short. He laughed with his whole self, cried with all his heart, and loved deeper than I have ever experienced. He would get his face so close to mine when he had something specific he needed me to hear. It was almost as if he looked into my soul, making sure that I would never forget. He was giving me the chance to memorize his precious little face. I am so thankful that I did.

Every moment we had him, all three-and-a-half years, was an absolute joy. He loved his "Chan Man," his brother and best friend who wouldn't allow him to get away with anything. He loved his "Bubba," the best big brother a boy could have. Ramsey definitely had him wrapped around his finger. The three of them fought hard but loved harder. All three were all-boy.

Ramsey—today a fireman, tomorrow a ninja, but every day our precious little man!

With love,
Ramsey's Mommy

chapter one

From Mommy to Mom

There are a number of great housekeeping tips available online. However, I never thought I'd be searching for tips like this one.

According to Heloise:

> There are many different types of headstones, but if you know that the marker you want to clean is granite and that it's soiled with just dirt and mildew, here's a suggestion: First, protect any ceramic photographs or bronze fixtures by masking them, and protect the grass around the marker by covering it with newspapers. Then wet the stone with plain water. Next, mix a solution of 50 percent regular household bleach and 50 percent water, and scrub the stone, using only a nylon or fiber brush (do not use anything containing metal because it can scratch or leave fragments behind that can damage the granite surface). Let set for 20 to 30 minutes, then rinse with plain water.

If you do not know the type of stone, the cemetery management or the monument company may be able to tell you—and recommend the best cleaning product. Any abrasive or acidic cleaning agents can easily damage headstones with a glazed finish. For bronze markers, there are special cleaning kits (available from monument supply companies).[1]

I was not prepared for what was about to happen to me. But then again, how could you be prepared to choose burial plots and caskets for your toddler?

OH, WHAT ABOUT MY HEART?

At the funeral home we were told he could have a lady's casket rather than a child's size, if we preferred that. *Prefer? How can you even have a preference on something like this? And a vault? What on earth is that for?* This was our first time to have to make such decisions. We'd never had a death in the family. Even all the grandparents were still living! We had no idea how to walk this out.

While we were trying to choose the burial plot, they were trying to make a sale! The funeral home wanted to sell us three spots—one would be for my husband and one would be for me so we could be buried next to Ramsey. How

---

1 Heloise, "How to Care for Headstones," *Good Housekeeping*, http://www.goodhousekeeping.com/home/heloise/headstone-caring-oct01.

thoughtful. I remember gasping for air in disbelief that the lady was actually trying to sell us burial plots while we were heading into the building to choose a casket for our son.

A week after the burial, I realized I had not only lost a son—something else had shifted in my life. My role within the family had changed. As a mother of little ones, you are "Mommy." There are certain duties a *mommy* has that a *mom* graduates from. Toddlers need help bathing and washing their hair. They need help tying their shoes and cutting their steak. They cannot transition from pull-ups to big-boy undies without someone's help. With Ramsey being three-and-a-half years old, I was certain this transition to "momhood" would not take place for another four years; but, suddenly and against my will, I was in this new place. I was a mom.

I lay in the floor that morning pleading with God to bring understanding and clarity to this new position. I was not yet ready to trade in my mommy-card at the age of thirty-eight for the more mature one of mom, yet my circumstances were forcing an abrupt change.

My position not only changed within our home but also within my sphere of influence. I was no longer the same woman with the same relationships. My friends were afraid—of what to say, how to act, and how to comfort me.

I believe my experience uncovered tremendous fear in the hearts of many young moms I knew. After all, the thought of burying a child is more than most can entertain. It is so easy to isolate yourself from the possibility of this type of tragedy ever touching your family, and then suddenly it happens just a little too close to home.

I remember hearing about such devastation on the news and immediately thinking, *That would never happen to me because I would never allow my young children by the poolside, alone.* But it did. I was no more immune to tragedy than the next mom.

I believe this bubble of supposed protection that many surround themselves and their families with oftentimes has to do with their religion. People will grab hold of the mindset that they are somehow protected from heartbreaking circumstances because they have a relationship with their Creator.

In reality, no one is completely protected from pain and heartbreak. It's not a result of an uncaring God, but a result of the Fall by the original parents, Adam and Eve. At that moment death, sin, pain, and suffering entered. So when Ramsey drowned, many acquaintances exited our lives because it unveiled a truth they had never allowed themselves to consider: Someone can be serving God and still bury a child.

In a state of surrender—full of fear, anger, frustration and desperation—I asked the question: "What am I supposed to do now Lord?"

In a state of surrender—full of fear, anger, frustration, and desperation—I asked this question: "What am I supposed to do now, Lord?!" I had not planned on a future where I no longer had my little one in the home. He'd grow up, sure. But now he was gone.

Everything in my world was turned upside down. I had to somehow determine how to carry on as a wife and a mom to two sons, rather than three—but what would that look like? My husband described it best when he said, "The veil is removed. You feel that your life is going in one direction, and now the veil of what you thought you would be changes into who you are currently." The reality for us was that this metamorphosis took place within an hour's time.

And what about the tombstone? I had no idea there were so many choices. We spent hours looking through magazines and walking the cemetery to see if there was anything we liked. Some lay flat on the ground and some stood up; some had vases for flowers and some didn't. Some were brass and some were granite and some were black and some were white, and the choices were overwhelming—but we felt we had to choose the *perfect one* because it would be a forever reminder of our child. Oh, you get to choose a little quote, or perhaps you can make one up to serve as a tribute to that child. But honestly, what could you possibly say that would be adequate?

Choosing the burial spot was difficult enough and was made even more painful by the salesperson pushing us to buy the extra spots next to Ramsey's, which we did. That and the pressure of choosing the perfect headstone placed overwhelming pressure on these young parents. We felt nothing was good enough and that it was our last chance to honor him, so we put unbelievable stress upon ourselves.

I kept thinking, *I should have a toddler, but instead I am searching for headstones and ways to care for it. This is just not right!* The reality was that I would never again drive to Mom's Morning Out to pick up my son. I would not have the opportunity to pack his lunch, allowing him to choose his "jucee" flavor of the day. There would be no more reading of *The Gingerbread Man* or *Bedtime Stories* by Rudyard Kipling. No more singing old spirituals at bedtime. No more swords, tricycles, army men, or "Little Bear" videos. No more chocolate-lined mouths to wipe clean. No more butterfly kisses.

God, help my heart.

You don't have to order the stone prior to burial—and we didn't—but the thought of having his name on a cheap, temporary stone was too much for us, and we felt we had to take care of it right away.

It took about eight weeks for his headstone to be delivered to the cemetery office. Meanwhile, Ramsey had a temporary nameplate. It almost felt as if his passing was insignificant until he had a headstone. But once it was put in place—seeing it in concrete was like being hit in the gut with a baseball bat. Reality hit like no other time!

I was flooded with emotion and uncontrollable tears. All a of sudden I couldn't remember where I'd placed my car keys. My children had to ask me three and four times for lunch. I could barely function. I fluctuated between moping and disbelieving, to uncontrollable weeping in the grocery without any notice or triggers. I had lost my center.

The next year and a half turned out to be one of the most suffocating periods of my life. There were days I would cry out, begging God to allow me to stay in bed. I didn't want to get up and face another day. I didn't feel I could handle any more pain. I just wanted to wake up from my sleep and find out this was all just a horrible dream.

There were also days when I was certain He was scooping me out of the bed and planting my feet firmly on the floor. This went on day after day . . . month after month.

THE CHOICE WAS MINE

Every morning Jay would get the boys ready for school and get them on the bus while I stayed in bed. I cried myself to sleep every night, and when the sun came out in the morning, I hid under the covers. The depression was real, blanketing me. Sometimes I was unable to breathe. The grieving felt more like fear.

My goal was to wake up by 8:00, and shower and get dressed by noon.

I was afraid to stay home alone because the minute everyone left, visions of the drowning would flood my mind. I could hear the screams and see the frantic looks on everyone's faces. So Jay insisted that I get up and get out. My goal was to wake up by 8:00, and shower and get dressed by noon. There would be many tears in between.

Every day my husband would try to get me to meet him for lunch. It took all the effort I had to get out of the house every day.

I needed comfort. I needed peace. But there were some days when I could barely speak His name as I cried out for help. I made daily attempts to read the Word and to pray, but most times, "Juhhh . . ." was all I could utter into the pain-filled silence. Jesus heard me anyway.

I had a decision to make. I could either walk through this experience and somehow become a better person, or I could choose to become bitter.

THERE IS NO PLAN B

Even with the heavy burden I now carried, I was completely committed to the God that I served. There was no second-guessing where I stood in my relationship with Him. After all, who else was going to help me through this?

I was often reminded of the woman with the issue of blood from Luke 8:40–48:

> Now when Jesus returned, the crowd welcomed him, for they were all waiting for him. And there came a man named Jairus, who was a ruler of the synagogue. And falling at Jesus' feet, he implored him to come to his house, for he had an only daughter, about twelve years of age, and she was dying. As Jesus went, the people pressed around him. And there was a woman who had had a discharge of blood for twelve years, and though she had spent all her livelihood on

physicians, she could not be healed by anyone. She came up behind him and touched the fringe of his garment, and immediately her discharge of blood ceased. And Jesus said, "Who was it that touched me?" When all denied it, Peter said, "Master, the crowds surround you and are pressing in on you!" But Jesus said, "Someone touched me, for I perceive that power has gone out from me." And when the woman saw that she was not hidden, she came trembling, and falling down before him declared in the presence of all the people why she had touched him, and how she had been immediately healed. And he said to her, "Daughter, your faith has made you well; go in peace."

Now, this woman was broken. According to Scripture, she had endured twelve years of bleeding. She had tried everything medically and had exhausted all of her finances trying to find a cure. According to the Talmud, there were eleven procedures to be used to address the issue of bleeding. We have to assume that this woman had already attempted them all without success.

Leviticus 15:19 states, "When a woman has a discharge, and the discharge in her body is blood, she shall be in her menstrual impurity for seven days, and whoever touches her shall be unclean until the evening." This meant that wherever the bleeding woman lay or sat was unclean, as well. If she accidently bumped into someone, they would probably scream, "Unclean! Unclean!" It would not be long before everyone would know of her illness and abandon her.

Can you imagine the devastation in this? We are not told from the Scriptures if she had children but if she did, she was unable to be with them. She could not have a normal relationship with her husband. Many theologians believe her husband divorced her after this length of sickness. The side effects of this type of issue also include loss of strength and weight. So she was feeling weak, rejected, broken, isolated, with no hope of winning.

I believe this woman would know and understand how I felt. She felt completely isolated because no one could understand the depth of her pain and brokenness, and they did not want to get close to her infirmity for fear it would be transferred to them. She was hopeless, desperate, and helpless. I was right there, too.

Desperation will cause you to go where you shouldn't, and ask for what you normally are not brave enough to ask; but it also causes you to believe when you have no natural reason to do so.

Desperation will cause you to go where you shouldn't, and ask for what you normally are not brave enough to ask; but it also causes you to believe when you have no natural reason to do so. So, she decided to do what her culture said she couldn't.

This unclean woman made a decision that she was not going to remain in that place any longer. She had heard about a man the people called Jesus, and how He was going around healing people's brokenness. As an unclean woman, she knew it would be impossible to get to him; but she had resolve and devised a plan. For her, there was no Plan B.

She elbowed her way through the crowd toward Him. Since all the townspeople knew of her and her illness, she probably disguised herself to get near the Rabbi. As she moved closer to Him, she shoved and pushed and finally, "She came up behind him and touched the fringe of his garment, and immediately her discharge of blood ceased" (Luke 8:44). Yes, she was healed! She touched the hem of His garment and was healed in an instant.

So, why the hem? The priests were anointed and the overflow of the oil eventually gathered at the hem of the garment. Many theologians believe this is the reason she fell at His feet, in an attempt to touch the most anointed place.

I believe that what you do in private, you will also do publicly as an overflow of your relationship with God. I believe she fell at His feet because it was the location she was most familiar with. There is such confidence in knowing that if you are desperate and cannot utter His name, simply falling at His feet releases hope overflowing into the most painful crevices of your heart. At His feet was where I would spend the next season—being in His presence, and learning to better hear His voice. There I would learn to trust like I never had before, and it was there I began to be healed by the Rabbi.

I was also reminded of the Samaritan woman, the woman at the well from the account of John 4:6–42. In verse 16, "Jesus said to her, 'Go, call your husband, and come here.' The woman answered him, 'I have no husband.' Jesus said to her, 'You are right in saying, "I have no husband"; for you have had five husbands, and the one you now have is not your husband. What you have said is true.'"

Her previous five husbands either died or divorced her. She was broken. She was lost. She was hurting. She was empty and desperate, ashamed and isolated. Some women never recover from one episode of this type of rejection, yet this woman was walking the path of five times that. Her once-beautiful body was now broken and weary, weighed down and aged by grief and devastation.

I share the accounts of these two broken women because I could see myself so clearly in them. I felt isolated, hopeless, and weary. Had I somehow caused my suffering?

Did I bring this on myself?

Was it all my fault?

BAD WORDS

Soon after the accident, I was on a rare outing to the grocery store when a woman I knew stopped to talk to me. I have to believe she meant well, but she didn't choose her words wisely and asked, "How on earth could this have happened? Weren't you watching him?" My heart was crushed again.

We made a family decision following that episode to buy groceries in the neighboring city, about thirty minutes away. People were just not safe anymore. Either they were aware of Ramsey's drowning and would say hurtful things in front of our other two children, or they were unaware of the circumstances and inquired to his whereabouts. Either way, we were far too fragile at this time to trust people with our family. The comments being made to me, especially, caused me to question myself, which only opened the door to guilt and more depression.

The worse I felt, the more I looked to the strong women in the Bible. Both women—the woman with the issue of blood and the woman at the well—walked through devastation in their lives. One was completely isolated from everything and everyone who was familiar to her. For twelve years she was in hiding. I was in hiding, too, because I could not face the reality of truth. She was embarrassed by the glares and the talk. It was the same for me. Everyone knew my story. Everyone glared and talked under their breath. I knew it. I could feel it. I could also hear their whispers.

One day, after battling for twelve years, the woman with the issue of blood decided she was done. She was tired of hiding. She was tired of the stares and tired of the whispers.

The Scriptures tell us that the Samaritan woman went to draw water in the heat of the day. This was a task that was typically handled in the evening after the sun went down. She was sneaking out in the heat to avoid the people.

If you're breathing, you know it is possible to be judgmental without ever speaking a word. There are looks and body languages far more communicative than thoughts spoken aloud. And this woman—she was definitely the talk of the town. Everyone knew of her multiple husbands. Whether they died or divorced her, either her fault or not, the fingers pointed toward her brought more shame than she could bear.

God saw both of these women in the midst of their greatest suffering. The woman with the blood issue did everything she could medically to stop the pain, and she made the decision that she was not going to stay in that place another day.

The Samaritan woman felt completely hopeless with no way out. Whether or not she contributed to the divorces, deaths, or abandonments, she surely carried the shame. She decided to fly under the radar and do the best she could to survive. Both women were faced with transitions they could not control.

Just like them, I had a decision to make. I had been forced into transition and had no control. How would I respond? Would I choose bitter or better? Would I continue hiding and choose to stay on the fringes of society in hopes I would survive somehow? Or would I rise up and make the decision to win in the midst of the devastating truth that I was suddenly a "mom"?

HIDE AND SEEK

Despite the whispers and words from members of the community, we had tremendous support from our church family. The pastors and leaders surrounded us physically, as well as in prayer. The shock of our circumstance touched the hearts of our church, and they wept alongside us and gave support as best they knew how. They gave us space to grieve and mourn without putting any expectations on us regarding what it should look like. They simply loved us from afar, yet close enough for us to know we were surrounded by them.

They allowed us to hide for a season, which was exactly what we needed. The love our church family showed us and the space that they allowed us are what helped us to walk through the process in a healthy way.

During this hiding season, which lasted about a year, I was unable to stay alone. Fear gripped my heart. The thought of sending our middle son, Chandler, back to public school was more than I could bear, so Jay and I decided to homeschool him for a year. He was so insecure at this time and so was I. He required constant attention and did not want us out of his sight.

Honestly, I didn't want my family away from me either. We'd experienced such loss. Such devastation. All I wanted—all we wanted—was to go back to how things used to be. Before we knew death. Before we knew about children's caskets. Before that one Friday afternoon.

chapter two

Because of This . . . I Am

On Friday, May 26, 2000, our youngest son, Ramsey, drowned in our backyard pool at the age of three and a half.

OUR NORMAL SCHEDULE
WAS INTERRUPTED

Benjamin, our oldest son, was in the midst of preseason practices with a traveling baseball team, but Jay and I were not happy about his coach. This guy had rotten fruit, and we did not want him sowing into our son.

We have never allowed our children to quit anything. If they decided to do something, we stood firm that that they would complete the assignment. Well, we were at practice one day, and the coach was comparing the players and using language that was surely inappropriate for twelve-year-old boys. As a family, we decided we would allow Benjamin to step back from this particular coach.

We removed him from the team at the beginning of the week of May 22. The games had already been scheduled for the season, and his first game would have been on May 26. We were supposed to be at the ball field that afternoon.

EVER HAD A DEBT
YOU COULDN'T PAY?

After my husband graduated from veterinary school in the late 1980s, we found ourselves caught up in emotion and expectation. We made poor choices in buying a practice in Northport, Alabama, that was overvalued. The practice could not generate enough income to support the inflated payments; and that, along with a shutdown of one of the local major industries that was a huge part of our clientele, was more than the business could carry.

After three years, we chose to give the practice back to the original owner in 1991. We assumed the pain was over, since we had made the purchase through owner-financing. We assumed we could walk away.

We moved to Huntsville, Alabama, to be closer to our family, and my husband took a veterinary position there with a $40,000 cut in pay. We moved with nothing more than hope in our hearts for a fresh start.

I tried and tried to find a job. With three children, the expenses of childcare and after-school care made it difficult, but I continued to look. I eventually found work, but we couldn't get ahead because of the overall costs of raising three children. It seemed impossible.

We had been in the new location just a few months when our accountant called. She, with a bit of laughter in her voice, said, "You owe the IRS $75,000 as a result of recapture." *What—$75,000? Recapture? What does that mean?*

Well, we were about to find out.

As a result of the way the accountant calculated our taxes, giving us every tax advantage on the front end rather than spreading it throughout the repayment period, we now owed $75,000. Money we certainly didn't have.

We were in a new city. Jay had taken a $40,000 pay cut. We had pretty much lost everything we had. Now we were looking at debt with no way of survival.

The hate letters from the IRS began almost immediately.

IT WAS A MIRACLE

On Friday morning, May 26, 2000, we received a phone call—a couple wanted to take us to lunch. We were just happy to get away for a moment and never could have imagined their intent. They had heard about our tax troubles and they came to lunch with two checks in hand. The two checks totaled the amount we needed to pay off the IRS tax debt. The *exact* amount.

Well, that changed everything!

Benjamin and Chandler were still at school, and since

Benjamin had stepped away from baseball, we had the afternoon free. Ramsey would stay at the office with Linda, one of my husband's employees, while we went to the tax office to pay our debt in full. Oh, it was a great day. We had money in our hands and hope in our hearts!

As we were leaving, we saw Linda pushing Ramsey in a wheelbarrow, up and down the hills, all across the yard, and we could hear him giggling. It was the sweetest thing! We pulled away knowing he was happy and all was well.

Thirty minutes later, we arrived at the Internal Revenue Service office in Huntsville with our two checks in hand. The drive time allowed us to dream again about how the noose would be removed from our necks and how we could give our children a different life—the one we wanted them to have. One that would be filled with laughter rather than the stress and worry they had seen on their parents' faces recently. Would this fresh start allow us to relocate, or would we stay in the Madison area? The excitement of a clean slate was almost more than these two young parents could contain. We had carried this IRS weight for the last nine years and it showed on our countenances. What would this new season be like? Endless possibilities lay before us.

We walked into the Internal Revenue Office and proudly told them we were there to pay off our tax liens. We laid those two checks down on the counter and received our stamped "Paid in Full" receipt. God had delivered and answered our prayers. This debt had crushed the life out us for so many years, and now . . . boom! Just like that! He answered.

When we pulled into the office, we found Linda and Ramsey chasing bugs in the backyard at the clinic. I remember the huge smile on Ramsey's face!

Jay walked into the office to finish off the day, and I loaded Ramsey into the car seat and headed home.

HOME SWEET HOME

We lived next door to a Baptist church. Our home was a beautiful two-story with a detached garage and a little white-picket fence connecting the garage to the house. A huge magnolia tree in the front faced the street.

We had a lovely front yard, perfect for boys to play ball, ride their bikes, and chase bugs, but what was more perfect was the backyard. It was truly a child's dream place. There was a pool with a cascading waterfall, a trampoline, a swing set, a jungle gym for climbing, motorized riding toys, tricycles, bicycles, balls, bats . . . you name it! A five-foot white-picket fence surrounded the backyard. There was also a huge deck with three wooden steps that led down to the concrete pad. The pad was about five feet wide surrounding the pool, and the rest of the backyard, where all the toys were, was covered in luscious green grass.

My favorite part of the house was the breezeway. On one side, there was a beautiful glass door with five brick steps leading down to a large concrete landing. On the other was a fence near the magnolia tree, which blocked the view of the street. White latticework surrounded the entrance from the sidewalk and the pool, and in the middle sat my little bistro set. My happy place. I kept it cozy with a candle, a notepad, and a Bible. Sometimes flowers.

The breezeway was not just a beautiful place. It was not just a place of peace filled with the aroma of magnolia blossoms. No, it was something much greater. It was the place where I met with Jesus daily. I would get up at 4:00 in the morning, grab my Bible, notepad, coffee, and lighter, and begin by lighting the candle.

Even in the winter, I sat on those brick steps wrapped in a blanket with a space heater plugged in, the snow falling just beyond the magnolia tree. I also remember sitting there in the midst of the summer heat with a fan blowing just to keep cool enough. It was my hiding place, my familiar place. I could pray harder, love deeper, and worship longer in this breezeway. It was my favorite hideaway, with the smell of magnolia always present.

As much as I loved my breezeway, Ramsey loved school buses. We would stand at the door in the morning and watch the school bus picking up the children, and we did the same in the afternoons. The church owned six buses and they would occasionally park them at the back of their parking lot where Ramsey could see them, visible from our hideaway. He would talk about the buses all day. You know, "The wheels on the bus go round and round, round and round, round and round, the wheels on the bus go round and round, all day long."

A MILLION POPSICLES

We had just paid the IRS and were driving home from Jay's office when Ramsey asked for a popsicle. I needed to pick up a few things at the grocery, so we decided to make a stop. We went inside, I put him in the cart, and we quickly made our way through the store, picking up a few items and saving the popsicle aisle for last.

Finally on the ice cream aisle, I pushed him through. He looked in all the cases and chose one box of Bomb Pops®. His favorite. I said, "Go ahead and pick out several." You see, for the first time in three years, I was really beginning to sense the rope releasing from my throat concerning our finances. After all, they were just popsicles. He chose several more, and we got to the cash register with the few items we needed and six boxes of Bomb Pops®.

Back home, Ramsey helped me carry the bags inside. I checked on Benjamin, who had come home from school with food poisoning. Chandler was watching television, and Ramsey yelled, "Come on, bubba, we got a million popsicles!" It was a beautiful afternoon. The sun was shining—an absolutely perfect day outside.

The two boys chose their popsicles and decided to sit on the deck to enjoy them. Ramsey insisted on having the blow dryer going while they ate popsicles on the deck so they could stay warm. It had become a Waite tradition to have popsicles and blow dryers, simultaneously.

Ramsey would dip his toes in the water (he would not

get in) whenever we would have a family pool day, and
the boys would splash him while he stood on the side. He
would throw a water bomb to the boys in the pool, and
they would allow the bomb ball to soak up a ton of water.
When they threw it back to him, water would go everywhere and he would giggle so hard. That is how he became
wet, and how the blow dryer became a common fixture in
our family.

I put a few dishes in the dishwasher as I watched them
through the kitchen window eating their popsicles, and I
could hear their giggles. When I walked upstairs to get the
laundry from Ramsey's bedroom, his room looked just as
it did every day—clothes strewn across the floor, mixed in
with a gazillion toys. I picked up the clothes, put them in the
basket, and as I did so, Chandler came walking up the stairs
and into his bedroom. Ramsey was not with him. I asked
where he was, and Chandler said he was finishing his popsicle
on the deck. I picked up the scattered toys and placed them
in the large toy box. I straightened his little bed, and down
the stairs I went with the basket of clothes.

I walked into the laundry room just off the kitchen, threw
in a load of clothes, and looked out the window. I didn't see
Ramsey sitting at the table or on the deck, but I didn't panic
because of the awesome backyard I described. He was playing somewhere.

I opened the door, walked onto the deck, and looked
around the yard. I still didn't see him. I called his name a
couple of times and got no response. I looked in the pool

to make sure, and he was not there; so I walked inside the kitchen with peace in my heart. Ramsey didn't like the pool anyway, so I was not surprised that he was not near it.

I'll never know the reason he didn't like the pool, although he loved baths. This is just another reason why I feel that he knew his time this side of heaven would be short.

As for pool rules, the boys were not allowed to get in the pool without an adult there. Benjamin, twelve years old, was not allowed to swim alone either, especially if there were friends over. We had very strict rules about this.

Now it had been about five minutes, and I still couldn't find Ramsey. I walked in the kitchen calling his name. I walked through the entire downstairs with no answer. I yelled up the stairs and got no answer. I could hear the children's television and game system going while I checked all the rooms, but nothing. I began to get a little anxious.

I hurried down the stairs and into the backyard again, and called his name. I looked into the pool from the deck and he was nowhere to be found. When I looked over at the gate to the picket fence, it was closed. I ran back inside, through the breezeway, and into the detached garage that had a huge room upstairs filled with kid things. It was the only other place I knew to look, and I yelled his name in a voice that only a mother can. *"Ramsey, you better answer me now or I'm going to spank you. I am not playing. Answer me!"* Nothing. I ran up the stairs again to see if he was hiding from me. He'd never done that before, but I was beginning to panic.

The boys had no idea what was going on. Benjamin was

still in bed sick with food poisoning, and Chandler was still in his room playing video games.

By this point fear began to grip me. Suddenly, I remembered the school buses next door. *He loves buses!* I ran to all six buses, and only two were unlocked. I opened those two and ran down the rows, yelling his name, and still no answer.

I took off running toward the house, my heart beating out of my chest. As I stepped into the breezeway, I was stopped in my tracks, as if I had hit a brick wall. I heard these words: "Go back to the pool! Go back to the pool!" The voice was loud and so clear that I turned and looked behind me, thinking God was standing there. He said again, "Go back to the pool."

I said, "God, please no! Please not the pool!"

Over the years as I have shared this story, I have had so many people say to me that voice was the enemy . . . "That was not God!" But the Scriptures tell us in John 10:27 that we know our Father's voice. For those of you who have children, have you ever been shopping and you suddenly realize that your child has stepped out of your sight? You know that panicked feeling that you get in the pit of your stomach? I was right there. He knew what was happening inside my heart at that moment. He heard my desperate cry for help and He spoke!

I said, "God, please no! Please not the pool!"

The moment I entered the breezeway, I remember breathing in the most amazing smell of magnolia. It was almost as if the smell filled my nostrils and spoke peace into my spirit. I knew He was there. I knew He had spoken. I remember taking a huge cleansing breath of the magnolia (in the place that was most familiar to me, where I met Him every day) and taking that first step up the brick stairs. *God, help me! Please don't let him be in the pool!*

I went running onto the pool deck and I looked, but he was not there. Just as it was the three other times I had looked. I remember taking a huge breath of relief. I continued to walk down the three wooden steps leading to the concrete pad that surrounded the pool—and there he was. In the deep end, in eight feet of water! His little body was lying between the side of the pool closest to the house, and next to the drain. Now it was obvious why I could not see him from the top of the deck. I could not have seen him without looking over the side.

I've been swimming my whole life, so I jumped into the pool with my clothes and shoes on, but I could not get to him. I kept trying to dive down to him but I was panicking, and I couldn't get to him. I came up each time screaming, "Somebody help me! Somebody help me!" I remember crying out to God, "Send someone to help me!"

At the sound of my screaming from the poolside, both boys came running. The back door opened and Benjamin asked, "Mom! What is wrong?"

I screamed, "Ramsey is in the bottom of the pool!"

He came running across the deck, projectile vomiting from the food poisoning, then dove into the pool. The minute he hit the water, the enemy spoke to me and said, "Now I'm gonna take them both!"

I fell to the ground crying out to God like I never have in my life, but in a moment, Benjamin came up out of that water with Ramsey in his arms. I looked over and Chandler was standing on the deck watching all of this. He was only eight years old. He watched his mother screaming out to God, and his brother diving in the water, pulling up his baby brother from the deep end. That's a sight no child should ever have to witness.

I yelled for Chandler to bring me the phone as Benjamin started CPR. Chandler was literally wringing his hands. I handed Benjamin the phone, and the 911 dispatchers walked him through CPR, though he already knew the steps. I was still in a complete daze. I couldn't move. I was paralyzed.

I'd never seen her before but she said, "Ma'am, let's pray!"

Soon after the call, the ambulance arrived. The MedFlight helicopter landed in the church parking lot next door to our house about five minutes later. There had been no one at the church; it was about 6:45 p.m. on a Friday night. Now the backyard was filled with policemen, rescue workers, and neighbors.

I remember standing at the back of the fence, watching the chaos and crying out to God for help, when a woman walked over to me. I'd never seen her before but she said, "Ma'am, let's pray!" She began to pray the most beautiful prayer I had ever heard. The peace of God instantly settled upon my spirit. Then she said, "Come inside and let's get you some dry clothes on. Who can I call for you?"

I said, "Call my church!"

She called the church office across town, and someone immediately answered because they were having a Friday night prayer meeting. As soon as they got the call, they began to pray for our family.

Then this little woman helped me get dressed. She had the blackest hair I had ever seen. She was tiny, not even five feet tall. She had little hands. I will never forget her face. When I wanted her to go to the hospital with us, she was nowhere to be found. It was the strangest thing; no one else ever saw her.

This was before cell phones, and I remember wondering where Jay was. We tried calling him, but we were unable to reach him at work.

When he pulled up to the house that night, the entire front yard was covered with eight emergency vehicles. A helicopter was in the side yard. An ambulance was in the driveway. He described it by saying, "I have never been so scared and felt so helpless. I had no idea when I drove into my own driveway what had happened to my family. Who was hurt? What on earth had happened? I couldn't even imagine."

Jay got out of his truck and took off running toward the ambulance. He was yelling, "What has happened? What has happened?"

A stranger in the front yard said, "A little boy drowned in the pool." Jay didn't know which child it was. He didn't know if it was Ramsey or Chandler.

He pushed his way through the emergency workers in the ambulance and saw them working frantically on Ramsey. Jay moved out of the way, came out of the ambulance, and fell on his face in the yard. He lay there pleading for God to move. He bargained with Him! He begged!

Jay then got up and ran to find me. He came running up to me, and placed his hands on my shoulders. With his face close to mine and with tears pouring he said, "This is not your fault! Do you hear me? This is not your fault!" He made this comment to me not yet knowing what had even taken place. He didn't know if it was my fault or not.

> *"This is not your fault! Do you hear me? This is not your fault!"*

Ramsey was quickly moved from the ambulance in our driveway to the helicopter in the side yard, and was rushed to the hospital. Jay jumped into the ambulance once again and began streaming through the EKG strips, looking to see if there had been a heartbeat. He found nothing.

Our family loaded into our van and headed to the hospital. On the way, Jay repeated his words to me: "You love Ramsey. You would never want anything to happen to your boy. This is not your fault."

As we walked through the door of the hospital, there stood our pastor and his wife. I will never forget how relieved I was to see them standing there, with warm familiar faces. We were immediately rushed into a consultation room where we waited for about thirty minutes. We prayed. We cried. We begged for good news.

Finally the doctor walked in, looked us in the eyes, and began to cry. He said, "I am so sorry. There was nothing I could do."

THE BLAME GAME

It would be years before I would really understand the impact of Jay's statements to me that day. At the time, I blamed myself. I questioned myself. Each of the boys described how horrible my scream was upon seeing Ramsey in the pool. To this day, they say they can still hear my scream in their minds.

I would eventually find myself in a very deep and dark state of depression as I battled the questions in my mind and heart. But the Lord knew I would need to be reminded often of the truth: "It was not my fault!"

The Scriptures declare that each of us has a specific number of days and the truth is . . . that was the day for Ramsey. Yes, my heart still breaks, but that was the day that God chose to be his last on this earth, and I am convinced nothing could have stopped it.

Therefore, I Dance

*"In this sad world of ours, sorrow comes to all; and, to the young,
it comes with bitterest agony, because it takes them unawares
. . . Perfect relief is not possible, except with time. You can not
now realize that you will ever feel better. Is not this so? And
yet it is a mistake. You are sure to be happy again. To know
this, which is certainly true, will make you some less miserable
now. I have had experience enough to know what I say."*

—Abraham Lincoln
(This quote comes from a man who buried two sons.)

I preface this chapter by confessing that it was one I wanted
to delete multiple times. The reason? I was crushed by everyone's attempt to analyze and micromanage my grieving and
mourning process. I surely do not want to do that to anyone
else. So, please take this chapter and use it only as a guide if
you are questioning which stage you may currently be walking through, or what you may be experiencing—physically,
emotionally, or spiritually.

I am fairly transparent in this chapter concerning my

personal journey through grief and mourning. But please know that I did not get it all right, nor do I have any input concerning how you walk through yours. I release you right now to grieve and mourn your loss in any way that helps you find healing and wholeness for your heart. Be released.

WHAT IS TRAUMATIC GRIEF?

According to certified trauma specialists H. Norman Wright and Matt and Julie Woodley, there is a difference between when a loved one dies by natural death, which is difficult enough, and when the death is unexpected. For those who experience death without the opportunity to say good-bye, the grief is more intense and lasts longer. The specialists describe this experience as a form of shock, because there is no time to prepare. They share common descriptors that characterize reactions to traumatic grief:

- Unexpected: The surprise elements stun and shock. We feel dazed and disoriented.
- Uncontrollable: The event is beyond our abilities to change it. We feel powerless and vulnerable.
- Unimaginable: The horrific elements are not familiar to our way of life. Our frame of reference does not include what we are witnessing. We feel appalled and horrified.
- Unreal: The event is too strange to process. We see

but do not comprehend what we are seeing. We feel confused and disoriented.

- Unfair: We feel like victims who have done nothing to deserve this tragedy. We feel hurt, puzzled, angry, fearful.
- Unforgiveable: We need to blame someone or something. What do we do with our anger, rage, and urge to punish? We feel powerless.
- Unprecedented: Nothing like this has happened before. We don't have a script to follow. We feel directionless.
- Unprepared: We have not perceived a reason to ready ourselves for an unimaginable catastrophe. Our defense mechanisms may be inadequate to handle the demand. We feel overwhelmed.
- Uncertainty: We do not fully know the long-range effect on ourselves, our families, or jobs, or future, and the future of our offspring. We feel ambivalent and torn between hope and fear.[2]

Counselors told me that the pain and suffering is far greater if there are little or no answers to the tragedy.

Counselors told me that the pain and suffering is far greater if there are little or no answers to the tragedy. Ramsey was afraid of the water. He very seldom got into the pool, even if the whole family went in for

2 H. Norman Wright, Matt Woodley, and Julie Woodley, *Finding Hope When Life Goes Wrong* (Grand Rapids: Revell, 2008), 95.

a play day. He would wander the outskirts on his tricycle or climb the jungle gym or jump on the trampoline, but for him to actually come into the water was very rare. I remember a few times when he played in the waterfall, allowing it to gently sprinkle on his head, but only if I held him in my arms. So how could he have fallen in? There were several toys near the poolside. Did he trip over one? How could it have happened?

Dazed and disoriented, vulnerable and powerless, devastated and confused, fearful, overwhelmed, and helpless only begin to touch the surface of the emotions that I felt. I remember hurting in places I could not even touch. I felt like a hollow shell but with indescribable, deep pain. I would attempt to sleep and as soon as my eyes would close, the horrendous sight of how I found Ramsey would invade my mind.

A counselor described my grief as "unbearable pain that only intensifies." I believe she said it best. As a mother who buried a child, I found this to be the best description of the overwhelming flood of emotions that surrounded me, only increased by the tsunami of pain that cannot be controlled.

I was out of options and remember one day screaming out loud, "Peace, be still!" I could not stop the chaos in my mind. I shouted again, "Peace, be still!" Suddenly, I realized I was surrounded by calm that I could not imagine. Sometimes you simply need to tap into a Scripture that directly speaks to your circumstance and allow it to come alive.

STAGES OF GRIEF

According to counselors there are various stages of grief, and there is a phase that many have labeled "letting go."[3] I remember the first time I heard this phrase fear gripped my heart and then anger followed shortly. I was afraid that if I did not think of Ramsey multiple times throughout the day, that I might somehow forget the details of him: his smile, his chocolate-brown eyes, his chubby cheeks and hands. Then I was angry because "letting go" meant forgetting, at least to me, and why would anyone expect me to just "let go" of my son? "Letting go" ranked right up there with "just get over it" for me. I was offended by both these comments, and you should be as well.

Now I understand that it is not the memories that are being forgotten. It is realizing what needs to be "let go" of. Perhaps it is regrets, unfulfilled expectations, anger, the lifestyle you used to have, or even a routine. There is insecurity in letting go but a greater security in embracing life.[4] This was a very difficult place to be. For me, I had to get past the phrase "letting go" and choose to embrace what I had left. The past was the past, and I could not do anything to change it. My present and

I was afraid that if I did not think of Ramsey multiple times throughout the day, that I might somehow forget the details of him: his smile, his chocolate-brown eyes, his chubby cheeks and hands.

3   Ibid.

4   Joyce Rupp, *Praying Our Goodbyes* (New York: Ivy, 1988), 94–97.

my future suddenly shifted. I had to choose to embrace my new life.

GRIEVING DIFFERENTLY

My husband's grief was a bit more outward than mine. He experienced anger. He spends his days saving creatures; yet when his son was in the bottom of the pool, he had no opportunity to step in and save him. This was the most difficult part for Jay. There is such a helpless feeling that surrounds when you know you might have made a significant difference in the outcome, had you been there. But it was just not in the plan.

He really felt he had let Ramsey down, as did Benjamin, our oldest son. The truth is: nothing could have stopped the drowning that Friday evening, in my opinion.

It would have been easy to take on the guilt of this incident individually—the "what ifs," the "I shoulda beens," and the "I shouldn't haves"—but the reality is that by entertaining those guilt-ridden thoughts, there could have been no healthy grieving process for our family. We had to find peace in knowing that He is God and we are not. He is Sovereign. His plan will always be greater than ours.

I chose my friend, Maureen Broderson, Professor at The King's University–Van Nuys, California, as a supporting authority on this topic. She teaches the course "Grief Counseling: Effective Ministry to those Suffering Death,

Divorce, or Dying," and she beautifully addresses the impact of grief on the physical body. She describes what to expect during the process of grieving, and the hope that we have for the future: "Grieving is a unique and often prolonged event taking an immense toll on the human body. It is normal for grieving individuals to be focused on their emotions as they learn to live with their loss. It is critical that grieving individuals be observed for any symptoms of physical illness or deterioration."[5] She offers a list of physical expressions or conditions of grief:

- Sighing
- Crying/weeping
- Loss or increase of appetite
- Weight loss or weight gain
- Upset stomach as stress shuts down digestive activity
- Dry mouth as fluids are diverted from nonessential locations. This can cause spasms of the throat muscles, making it difficult to swallow.
- Easily startled
- Anxiety
- Shortness of breath or rapid breathing
- Sleep disturbances
- Cool, clammy or sweaty skin and/or tightness of scalp
- Fatigue

5   Maureen Broderson, "Grief Counseling: Effective Ministry to those Suffering Death, Divorce, or Dying," course at The King's University–Van Nuys, California.

- Depression
- Tightness in chest
- High blood pressure
- Heart palpitations
- Lowered immune system
- Missed menstrual cycle
- Complications related to pre-existing health conditions[6]

I experienced sixteen of the nineteen physical conditions that Broderson mentioned. The effects upon my physical body meant grief surely was taking its toll. Not only was I battling the flood of emotions in my mind, but also the sixteen physical symptoms; and the fear that surrounded me as a result of seeing my son in the pool was almost paralyzing. I remember one night being convinced that I was having a heart attack because the pain in my chest and the tightness was unbearable. I remember being unable to breathe and thinking that surely I would pass. These physical symptoms alone are debilitating.

Broderson continues by describing four major categories of loss and explains the intensity of loss that you feel is proportionate to the "replaceability" of who or what you have lost.

---

6   See National Institute of Mental Health, www.nimh.nih.gov; American Institute for Cognitive Therapy, www.cognitivetherapynyc.com; National Mental Health Association, www.nmha.org; The American Institute of Stress, www.stress.org; American Academy of Child and Adolescent Psychiatry, www.aacap.org; or Sarah Kliff, "Is Grief a Disease?" *Washington Post*, last modified May 14, 2012, http://www.washingtonpost.com/blogs/wonkblog/post/is-grief-a-disease/2012/05/14/gIQAnoFwOU_blog.html.

1. Loss of a significant loved or valued person;
2. Loss of part of the self—includes health, injury, reputation;
3. Loss of external projects: loss of property, financial resource, etc.; and
4. Developmental loss: a loss of relationship, i.e., "empty nest" syndrome, defeat, or function.

I remember counseling a young mother several years ago and as she sat looking into my eyes with such heartbreak over her husband's abandonment of their marriage, she said, "I feel that I am experiencing death." The moment she spoke, I realized her comment was on target. She was experiencing death. It was the death of her marriage, her family, her home, her finances, her dreams, her future, and her hopes of growing old with her high-school sweetheart. Suddenly, it all had been stripped from her.

In any community, regardless of location or affluence, there are families suffering loss. There are more layoffs, more foreclosures, and more retirement losses than I have ever observed. There is a whole generation that feels hopeless. They are educated with no hope of job placement. Many middle-aged workers are currently holding jobs that they are overqualified for with little hope of returning to their career fields. There is loss all around us. It is impossible to prepare for these types of devastating blows. Yes, it oftentimes feels unfair, yet the unfairness does not change the inevitable. Grieving and mourning are not simply for those who have buried a loved one. The process is real, and it covers a wide gamut of circumstances.

Dr. Glenn Schiraldi describes grief as the suffering associated with loss. It is about finding our own way again. I grieved the loss of my son, but I also grieved how my position changed within my home.

I grieved the loss of my son, but I also grieved how my position changed within my home.

Schiraldi defines mourning as "the process by which we explore, experience, express, and integrate our grief and adjust to a world with the loss."[7] I remember during the mourning process trying to learn how to "do life" now. I remember thinking: *Joy comes in the morning. Tomorrow I will have a plan of attack on how to survive this.* Tomorrow would come and nothing had changed. It was a daily process of just holding on to Him and choosing to place one foot in front of the other.

When Zig Ziglar's daughter passed away, he said, "When you're grieving, that's not the time to be brave. That's not the time to be strong. You need to be human."[8] This is so important. Everyone cannot handle the details of your loss, but I believe there will be somebody in your path who can. I just needed someone to listen.

---

7   Glenn R. Schiraldi, *The Post-Traumatic Stress Disorder Sourcebook: A Guide to Healing, Recovery, and Growth* (New York: McGraw-Hill, 2009), 249.

8   Samuel J. Hodges IV and Kathy Leonard, *Grieving with Hope: Finding Comfort as You Journey through Loss* (Grand Rapids: Baker Books, 2011), 18.

ALL EARS

My husband was the best listener of all and was always available to me. However, he was suffering through his own grieving process, trying to find healthy boundaries, and I was careful with how I loaded my burden on him. We all tried to be sensitive to the pain of each other. We each needed to grieve and walk through these most painful times without being judged and instructed on how to do it. I believe this outlet is normal and healthy.

I remember praying and asking God, "How do You expect me to survive this?"

He gently spoke, "Alongside of Me." I knew He saw my circumstance, and I also knew He was near. I did not have to measure my words with Him, although I did with almost everyone else.

During this time, a young mother from my church said, "You are really a strong woman for God to trust you with this." Well, I did *not* want to be strong. I did *not* want to be trusted. I just wanted my son! Although her comment cut me to the core, I knew that she truly meant no harm. What she did not understand was that I was *not* strong. I was holding on to Him with everything I had, trying to find my center. I had lost every form of familiarity that I had ever known. Strong? No. Desperately holding on to Him? Definitely.

The Fall of humanity has worked its defeating, disheartening, and discouraging effects in all of our lives. Oftentimes, what follows is complete despair and hopelessness. I am gently reminded from the Creation chapter that after the Fall, in the midst of punishment and judgment, God also gave hope! He pointed the people to Jesus Christ, His Son. Just as He pointed them to Him in the Book of Genesis, He continues to point us to Him presently as our ultimate hope. Whether we are facing the death of a loved one, the loss of a job, a failed marriage, a foreclosure on a home, or a fatal illness, do not allow fear to paralyze and immobilize your hope.

Apart from the Scriptures, there is no basis for hope.

Where do we go for hope? Apart from the Scriptures, there is no basis for hope.[9] There is no hope found in a temporary fix. Some turn to spending, some to drinking, some to drugs, and some choose to escape life and responsibility altogether. These always fail as a basis for hope. Dr. Jay Adams, a Christian counselor devoting his entire life to consoling the suffering, shared this truth—he has found no other useful tool to promote hope.

NOW YOU EXPECT ME TO DANCE?

A woman asked me, "So, when will He turn your mourning into dancing?" I didn't respond to her at that time because it really made me mad. She was implying that God would turn my mourning into a period of dancing. Yes, it ticked

9 Jay E. Adams, *The Christian Counselor's Manual: The Practice of Nouthetic Counseling* (Grand Rapids: Zondervan, 1973), 41.

me off, and I realized this particular Scripture really did not sit too well with me. The reason is that I could not imagine when or how after walking through this tragedy God would *ever* release dancing in me. So, why is this Scripture used so often in the circumstances of tragedy in an attempt to comfort, while leaving a poor taste in the hearer's mouth? Psalm 30:11–12 declares, "You have turned for me my mourning into dancing; you have loosed my sackcloth and clothed me with gladness, that my glory may sing your praise and not be silent. O Lord my God, I will give thanks to you forever!"

This psalm is categorized as a "Thanksgiving Song" of an individual. There are three typical elements to this type of song according to Dr. James Mays:

1. Praise addressed to the Lord that rehearses the cry for help in trouble and reports the Lord's response of hearing and help.
2. Summons to a community of worship to join the praise and testimony to them about the meaning of the deliverance for God's way and for the life of the saved.
3. Presentation of praise and/or sacrifice to keep promises made in a prayer for help.[10]

I have heard this passage taught multiple times—usually out of biblical context. When I heard how Dr. Mays shared

---

10 James L. Mays, *Interpretation: A Bible Commentary for Teaching and Preaching the Psalms* (Louisville: John Knox Press, 1994), 139.

some powerful truths concerning this particular text, I consulted with him to bring peace to my heart. Here is what I found:

- Psalm 30 is a prayer that is wholly praise; it is a praise that comes out of prayer.
- He references Psalm 30 as a prayer of thanks to be said *after* a prayer for help (already received) as in Psalm 6.
- In Psalm 30 the importance of praise to God is the basis and the goal of prayer (v. 12). Death was the danger from which the psalmist has been rescued (delivered).
- This Psalm demonstrates how prayer and praise can together become a rubric for holding the experiences of life in relation to God.

When you pray, first you ask for relief from the suffering and understanding for the grieving; then you thank Him for turning your mourning into dancing. In this context, that Psalm is consoling. In many others, such as when it is used as an icebreaker or advice, it is offensive.

During this several-year journey, I was able to redefine my identity as I changed my own mindset. I realized my life did not have to be tattooed with "the woman whose son drowned in her backyard pool," although the intrusive visions and memories tried to convince me—and onlookers—otherwise.

I also realized that I did not have to be known for my sins

or failures, nor my accomplishments. My identity resurfaced and I realized I was simply His. So, the dancing has to do with *how* He brought us through or how He *will* bring us through a particular situation. The dancing is a result of understanding and experiencing God's faithfulness to us. He has already delivered us, or He is in the process of delivering us.

I am currently practicing pirouettes in my heart because I trust and I believe. Therefore, I dance.

"Even though your heart is breaking and tears are clouding your eyes and staining your cheeks, God does give us something worth trusting in in tough times. And that's Him, and Him alone."

—JOSEPH STOWELL

chapter four

Job's Friends

As a little girl, I found my forever best friend. Her name was Kim. She was a few years younger than me. She had crazy, red, curly hair with about a million freckles and both front teeth missing. We would pretend to be mommies, rock stars, and runway models. We had arguments, we competed, we even pulled each other's hair on occasions—but at the end of the day, we were besties.

Over the years, we continued to do life together. We each married our high-school sweethearts and moved off to different colleges. She had three daughters. I had three sons. We have walked side-by-side as I buried my son and her young daughter survived cancer. There have been trying battles and floods of tears, all woven together with laughter throughout the past forty years of life's journey. There is no friendship to compare to this one.

When Kim heard the news of Ramsey's drowning, she jumped in her vehicle and drove to be by my side. She stepped up and stepped in from the moment she arrived. She sat at the poolside with my husband and me and wept as if Ramsey were her own son. She answered difficult questions so that I didn't have to, as the phone rang nonstop. She greeted those who dropped by the house unannounced. She was our liaison when we needed one—and she was definitely *not* like Job's friends.

WITH FRIENDS LIKE THESE . . .

"There was a man in the land of Uz whose name was Job, and that man was blameless and upright, one who feared God and turned away from evil. There were born to him seven sons and three daughters. He possessed 7,000 sheep, 3,000 camels, 500 yoke of oxen, and 500 female donkeys, and very many servants, so that this man was the greatest of all the people of the east" (Job 1:1–3).

Job was a very wealthy and blessed man. Suddenly he found himself without property, children, and health. Yet, he was a blameless and upright, God-fearing man. He was a wealthy landowner with a large household. He also knew how to connect with God.

"Now when Job's three friends heard of all this evil that had come upon him, they came each from his own place, Eliphaz the Temanite, Bildad the Shuhite, and Zophar the Naamathite. They made an appointment together to come to show him sympathy and comfort him. And when they saw him from a distance, they did not recognize him. And they raised their voices and wept, and they tore their robes and sprinkled dust on their heads toward heaven. And they sat with him on the ground seven days and seven nights, and no one spoke a word to him, for they saw that his suffering was very great" (Job 2:11–13). These were amazing friends. They entered into his suffering. They wept, mourned, and grieved alongside him. Then, they began to speak:

> Eliphaz said, "Remember: who that was innocent ever perished? Or where were the upright cut off?" (Job 4:7).
> Bildad said, "Does God pervert justice? Or does the Almighty pervert the right?" (Job 8:3).
> Zophar: "If you prepare your heart, you will stretch out your hands toward him. If iniquity is in your hand, put it far away, and let not injustice dwell in your tents. Surely then you will lift up your face without blemish; you will be secure and will not fear. You will forget your misery; you will remember it as waters that have passed away. And your life will be brighter than the noonday; its darkness will be like the morning. And you will feel secure, because there is hope; you will look around and take your rest in security. You will lie down, and none will make you afraid; many will court your favor. But the eyes of the wicked will fail; all way of escape will be lost to them, and their hope is to breathe their last." (Job 11:13–20)

These friends assumed that Job must have sinned, causing all this pain and suffering. They were confident that God was a fair judge and would reward all that is right. Their actions demonstrated love "in motion," but their words were judgmental, accusatory, and critical. Yet Job, in the midst of his darkest hour and in the agony of his greatest suffering, held on to God, believing. He was unmoved by their words.

ALL IN THE NAME OF THE LORD

I found myself in a place I never dreamed possible. The last thought on the mind of a mother of three sons, all perfectly healthy, is that within a blink of an eye (which in Hebrew means a half-blink) one of them would be gone. I was in a place of survival, as was the rest of my family. There would be many challenges beyond the death of our son—such as hurtful things people would say to us—that we were about to face. We

We were neither emotionally nor psychologically prepared to hear the comments that would be made to our family "all in the name of the Lord."

were neither emotionally nor psychologically prepared to hear the comments that would be made to our family "all in the name of the Lord."

These were the most common proposals made to us by Job's friends:

- God needed another angel in heaven.
- Why didn't you lay hands on him and raise him up?
- Only God knows what kind of adult your son would have turned out to be!
- Weren't you watching him? How could this happen?
- Just think about all those parents who have lost their only child. At least you have two others.
- You have got to pull yourself together for your family.
- Maybe it is better this way. If he had been revived, he would have surely been brain-dead and you would have spent your whole life caring for him with an infant mind.
- He was just an angel. He was not meant for this world.
- Well, you are still young enough to have another child.
- You have to be strong for your husband and your other two sons.
- I know how you feel.
- You two are such perfect parents. I can't understand the reason God would take your son from you and allow other children that are being abused to remain in the hands of their abusers.
- I am a miracle. When I was two years old, I fell into our backyard pool. My dad came running over just before I went completely under and jerked me out!
- He is in a better place now.
- Everything happens for a reason.
- God wouldn't give you more than He knows you can handle. You must be really strong.

- God giveth and God taketh away.
- At least you had him for three-and-a-half years.
- God is going to turn this around for good.
- The enemy snatched your son!
- At least you know you will see him again some day.
- I would never be able to live through burying one of my children.

"God needed another angel in heaven."

Ramsey did not become an angel when he passed, and neither does anyone else. Angels were all created at once. They do not have the power to reproduce in the normal fashion (Matthew 22:30), and there is no evidence of any new creations by God after the original creation of them (Genesis 2:2–3). I have heard this spoken from the pulpit in an attempt to comfort mourners when they are unable to supply adequate responses to their suffering. God does not take babies because He needs extra little helpers in heaven. There is no scriptural basis for this.

"You are going to have to find a way to get over this. Just step over it and embrace what you have left."

A pastor's wife said this to me. Honestly, I knew what she meant. She could not bear watching us suffer, but there is just no "getting over it" as much as outsiders desire this for you. Your suffering affects a lot of people, and some of those people are uncomfortable that what happened to you has just invaded their "safety zone," forcing them to consider their own vulnerability.

"Just think about all those parents who have lost their only child. At least you have two others."

I heard this statement made more than any of the others. It is impossible to claim that one human being could ever take the place of another one. Each child is unique. They have their own facial gestures; their own love language; their own cute habits; and each of these is beautifully individual. To make such a statement almost implies that all children are the same. God doesn't even make *snowflakes* the same. He is surely not going to make people identical. Even identical twins have different fingerprints!

According to Psalm 139:14, we are "fearfully and wonderfully made." Verse 15 declares that we are "intricately woven in the depths of the earth." He made each of His children beautifully unique and different, giving each of us our own identity. He loves color. He loves uniqueness. He loves diversity. He is the Master designer, and He has done a beautiful work in each of His creations.

"I know how you feel."

Please do not tell someone who just lost a child that you understand because you just buried your mother. Unless you have walked through the loss of a child, you cannot compare it to the loss of any other family member.

**"God wouldn't give you more than He knows
you can handle. You must be really strong."**

No! I was not strong, and I did not want to be strong.
I was never asked to walk this path. It was handed to me.
I questioned God multiple times about this—I was certain
He had chosen the wrong girl for this journey. I did not see
how it was possible to survive it.

**"Only God knows what kind of adult your
son would have turned out to be!"**

All I knew was a precious three-and-a-half-year-old boy
who was more in love with his mommy than he was with life
itself, and you are suggesting that he might have turned into
some sort of monster?

"The enemy snatched your son!"

Oh my! I have to admit that this one literally placed fear
within me and shook me to my core. As a matter of fact, I
had prayed within three hours of Ramsey's drowning that the
Lord would place angels about my children and protect them.
This was not a new type of prayer for me. I always prayed
and continue to pray protection about my family. However,
this day was different. I prayed, and Ramsey drowned. Now,
how am I supposed to trust God with my other two children
if the enemy can simply come in and snatch them? I found
myself with many sleepless nights as I struggled through my
own theology.

OUT OF CONTEXT
AND OUT OF CONTROL

Just when we would come up for air, Scriptures being taken out of context would be given to us. Romans 8:28 declares, "And we know that for those who love God all things work together for good, for those who are called according to his purpose." This particular verse was given to me more times than I care to share. It was one of those Scriptures that people easily delivered, with error in their interpretation and with little thought as to the impact that their error would have on someone suffering and grieving the loss of a child.

People said that God was going to use my suffering to bring many into the Kingdom. They told me I would be able to minister to others who would lose their children through tragedy. That sounds nice and all, but I was not interested in being *that woman*, and people continued to tell me that God took my son so that I could advance the Kingdom. It was not what a broken mother was interested in hearing, and God drowning children for any purpose is not comfort in any form. This goes against the very nature and character of God.

I studied this passage at great length and really appreciate the note given in the ESV Study Bible as clarification and interpretation of this particular verse. It states, "God weaves everything together for good for his children. The 'good' in this context does not refer to earthly comfort, but conformity to Christ (v. 29), closer fellowship with God, bearing good fruit for the kingdom, and final glorification

(v. 30)."[11] Wayne Grudem writes, "Paul affirms that God does work wisely in all the things that come into our lives, and that through all these things he advances us toward the goal of conformity to the image of Christ."[12]

Paul was not claiming in this verse that "all" things are good. He was not stating that a tragic death of a child was a positive happening somehow in disguise. Ramsey's passing was not good! That is what I wanted to shout from the rooftop.

God would work through this tragedy. And I would continue to try to find my way, as people would routinely hand me this verse.

I would then be given Job 1:21: "And he said, 'Naked I came from my mother's womb, and naked shall I return. The Lord gave, and the Lord has taken away; blessed be the name of the Lord.'" After much research, meditation, and study, I found this through Matthew Henry's Commentary: "God gave us our being, made us, and not we ourselves, gave us our wealth; it was not our own ingenuity or industry that enriched us, but God's blessing on our cares and endeavors; he gave us power to get wealth."[13] Job did not say, "God made me rich but Satan made me poor." He said, "He that gave has taken away." He that gave all may take as much as He pleases. God has given everything that I own to me. I am simply a steward of these things. I chose this thinking based

---

11 *The ESV Study Bible* (Wheaton, IL: Crossway, 2008), 2171.

12 Wayne Grudem, *Systematic Theology: An Introduction to Biblical Doctrine* (Grand Rapids: Zondervan, 1994), 194.

13 Matthew Henry, *An Exposition of All the Books of the Old and New Testaments, Volume 2* (London: W. Baynes, 1804), 524.

on my understanding, research, and unveiling by the Holy Spirit: Ramsey has returned to his right owner.

BROTHERLY LOVE

Ramsey passed away on a Friday evening, May 26, and my sister-in-law, Robin, was scheduled for surgery on the following Monday. I encouraged her to keep the appointment, as it was scheduled for many months in advance.

We buried Ramsey on Tuesday.

A week after the funeral, Robin asked my brother, Mike, to drive her to my church since she was unable to drive after the surgery. Even though it was about a twenty-minute drive, he agreed.

Robin had been praying for my brother's salvation for twenty-one years. She suggested that he sit in the parking lot or drive around while she came in to be with me, since she was certain he would not be interested in attending the service with her. Instead, he pulled into the parking lot and came inside.

That particular Sunday a missionary evangelist was visiting our church. It was our first service back after burying Ramsey, and it was my brother and sister-in-law's first visit to our church. While the message was being delivered, my brother cried uncontrollably. When the altar call was given he practically ran to the front, fell to his face, and gave his life to the Lord. It was a beautiful experience to witness.

Twenty-one years of praying and we were witnessing the fruit of those prayers.

There was much turmoil going on in Mike's life at the time of Ramsey's passing. I believe the overwhelming circumstances, along with the devastation of Ramsey's tragedy, pushed him to the foot of the cross. It would turn out to be one of the most powerful conversions I would witness to date.

I remember Mike having so many questions over the next few weeks. He wept and wept asking God the reason something so awful would be allowed to happen to two godly parents. Why would such a loving family be forced to walk through such devastation? He kept saying, "It's just not right. It's just not fair."

I would later have family members and friends tell me that Ramsey had to pass in order to bring my brother into the Kingdom. Surely I did not hear them correctly. I love my brother unconditionally, but I was not willing to give up my son for his salvation. It was not fair for God to do that to me.

He would never trade one soul for another.

Well, He did *not* do that to me. He would never trade one soul for another. This did not align with the character and nature of the God I serve. He is God Almighty. He could have simply spoken to my brother, causing him to respond. He could have performed a miracle before him, ultimately leading him to the cross. He did not need my son to pass away in order to get Mike's attention. Multiple circumstances aligned themselves, bringing my brother into the Kingdom; but Ramsey's passing was only indirectly connected to his decision.

NO WORDS, PLEASE

After reading the gut-wrenching list I shared earlier, you might be wondering what is the "right thing to say" in a circumstance such as this. Several comments come to my mind in response to this question. I recall two different women's statements and actions toward me the night of the wake.

The first one was from my church. I saw her and her husband coming toward us, and they wept uncontrollably. She looked me in the eyes and never spoke a word. She simply lent her shoulder to me for the moment. I remember the embrace so well. She held me and held me and held me, and allowed me to crumble in her arms. No words were ever exchanged.

The second woman looked at me and said, "I cannot imagine how you feel, but my heart is breaking with yours." These were some of the most beautiful and comforting words I heard during the painful year that would follow.

My husband has a large veterinary practice, and many of his clients would encourage him by sending cards and letters or making telephone calls over the upcoming year. These were more helpful than those people who seemed to need to make comments in person.

Benjamin and Chandler had friends at church and at

school who would surround them and comfort them. Benjamin's close confidante at this time was a girl from his youth group, Megan. She would be the one over the years to come who would always be those "ears" for him.

Chandler had a second-grade teacher, Miss Simmons. I remember looking up at the wake and seeing her standing there with tears streaming down her cheeks. She had a gift bag for Chandler that contained a golden-colored stuffed cat. Chandler clung to that cat every night at bedtime. Such comfort in such a small gesture.

Words can easily destroy an already broken heart and spirit.

There is so much to learn from this experience in "how to" and "how not to" respond to a similar circumstance. Words can easily destroy an already broken heart and spirit. More damage is done to lives, homes, and churches by the tongue than by any other means. May we use it rather to comfort, console, and soothe others as God intended. He would have us be His hands, His feet, and His voice in the midst of someone's suffering. He would have us share in the carrying of one another's burdens. I believe He would have us listen with empathy and move with compassion.

We are to follow Jesus' example by showing compassion in dealing with others. However, God's compassion went beyond feeling the emotion; it was always demonstrated by action. I say we make the decision to enter into the pain and share in the suffering. Jesus did!

LOVE IN ACTION

This choice to enter in with me was demonstrated by two ladies: Ruth and Joni. Over the several days following Ramsey's drowning, these two ladies from my church visited regularly. Whenever the two of them would arrive, the atmosphere in our home would change. They brought in food, flowers, and gifts for the children, but mostly . . . they brought in hope!

I recall sitting in a burgundy recliner this particular day when the doorbell rang. My mother answered and it was Joni and Ruth. Ruth reached down to hug me, and we cried uncontrollably for what felt to be thirty minutes. I would later find out that Ruth had also buried a child. She recognized the intensity of the pain and suffering that I was experiencing at that very moment. I felt her embrace in a way I had never experienced. It was a feeling I would never forget, yet one I never wanted to experience with another mom. It was as if God Himself had me surrounded and protected.

I can honestly say I experienced the love of Jesus from those two like I had never known. There was a depth in Joni's eyes whenever she looked at me that told me she was suffering alongside of me. She was helping me carry my burden. It was almost as if she gazed into my soul and shared a portion of her strength with me. They would show up with such love in their eyes and peace in their spirits that I knew Jesus had sent them to comfort me. The Holy Spirit was definitely comforting me; but in the physical, He was using Joni and Ruth.

It was through this experience with these two godly

women that I learned how to care for others, as He would have us do. I thought I understood serving those in need, but this relationship with Joni and with Ruth went much deeper than that. It was almost like deep crying out to deep within the body of Christ. It was exactly what I believe the Lord would have us do and be to one another.

There are times when the pain and the suffering felt too great to carry. I felt they were not only "holding up my arms" but also showing me how to place one foot in front of the other. Sometimes you cannot remember how to walk, due to a devastating blow in your life—and this was one of those times. It was not that I distrusted God with my pain; rather it was so paralyzing in the natural that He was sending people of strength to help us stand.

There was another woman, Jennifer, who played the violin on the praise team. I did not know her well, but I knew she was one of the intercessors of the church; and I knew that the prayer team met on Thursday mornings.

This particular day happened to be a Thursday. It was one of those days within the first two weeks when I felt I was not going to make it through the day. I called my church and asked for Jennifer's name and telephone number. When I called, she answered right away. I told her who I was and that I needed extra prayer that day. As I began to speak the tears came rolling. I cried and cried and cried and cried. This episode lasted for about fifteen minutes, and I could not contain the tears. It never occurred to me to simply hang up the telephone.

As I lay in the bedroom floor weeping, she held tight to her telephone. I could hear her praying and crying quietly on the other end of the line. She never attempted to stop me or to counsel me. She simply held the phone, wept alongside me, and prayed. That moment would forever change my heart. She would become one of my best friends and missionary companions in the upcoming years. I needed that gentle-spirited woman in my life at that time. She, like Ruth and Joni, had been used by God to show His love for me. He was literally making lifelong friendships that would forever impact me and would teach me how to minister to others at a depth He had demonstrated through them.

Although I've shared some difficult events and painful words spoken to my family and me, I also wanted to share how God sent His special agents alongside us to override some of the suffering. I am convinced that had God not sent Ruth, Joni, and Jennifer into my life at such a time, the journey would have been next to impossible. He knew exactly what His daughter needed, and He delivered.

Love without words is best. No instruction needed. Just embrace, weep alongside, and pray without ceasing.

chapter five

Bent. Broken. Bewildered.

So, where was Ramsey at that very moment? I would visit the cemetery, just to walk away with more questions and torment. I would lie on the ground envisioning his smile and listening for his giggles. I would remember the huge chocolate-outlined smile he would greet me with regularly.

I could no longer hear what man had to say concerning my son's passing, or the whereabouts of him at that very moment, or even what I might expect in the future. I had heard so many sermons throughout the years, and honestly, I could not find any peace in any of it. I needed answers for myself and I needed them straight from God, Himself.

STARVING FOR TRUTH

Over the next twelve months after Ramsey's passing, I surrounded myself with the Word for eight to ten hours a day. My children would leave for school and my husband for work each day. Sometimes, they would return to find me in the same position as I was when they had left. I would go without food or a shower, simply sitting in the floor, surrounded by tools in an attempt to find Him and answers!

I was in survival mode and desperate for a deeper understanding. I knew there were answers for me, and I knew where to find them. After all, "apart from the Scriptures," there is no basis for hope. I would dig through the Scriptures until I found resolve. The Holy Spirit was leading me daily as I cried out for answers. *Where is my son? Prove it. Why did this happen? It is just not fair to him or to us. We are good parents, and he was just a toddler. We love our children. We provide. We protect. We are raising them in the fear and admonition of the Lord just as we were instructed in Scripture. Why are we finding ourselves in this place? I need answers!*

BEGIN AT THE BEGINNING

I began at Genesis 1:1: "In the beginning, God created the heavens and the earth." To me, that meant He knew everything that happened to my family on that day. If He created it all, then He surely was aware of it all. I began to find promises in His Word just for me. I held on to:

- Psalm 34:18: "The Lord is near to the brokenhearted and saves the crushed in spirit." I have always been aware of God's love for me. Some people struggle with this truth, but for me, God has always revealed Himself in this area. I clung to this Scripture as a reminder that when my heart is crushed with no hope of recovery, He is nearby. He sends the Comforter. He provides my hope.

- Psalm 147:3: "He heals the brokenhearted and binds up their wounds." He promises to heal our hearts and to help us pick up the pieces. For me this means I will heal, in time, and He will help me carry on with what I have left. I am His daughter and He will respond to the need of my heart.

- Matthew 11:28–30: "Come to me, all who labor and are heavy laden, and I will give you rest. Take my yoke upon you, and learn from me, for I am gentle and lowly in heart, and you will find rest for your souls. For my yoke is easy, and my burden is light." When I considered the term *labor* I realized it meant "with great effort." The term *heavy laden* means "loaded to excess." I was there. It took great effort for me simply to function, and I was definitely feeling loaded to excess. I could not carry the burden. He was telling me, "Come, daughter, and I will give you rest from your physical and mental exhaustion."

"Take my yoke upon you, and learn from me, for I am gentle and lowly in heart, and you will find rest for your souls. For my yoke is easy, and my burden is light" (vv. 29–30). He was inviting me to wear His yoke! A yoke is made for two. He was asking me to allow Him to do the pulling and the carrying. This is what makes it easy and light. He is saying, "I see you are loaded to excess. I see you are physically and mentally exhausted. Connect with Me, My daughter . . . *Let* me carry you!" I needed to be carried. Jesus is saying, "Take My doctrine because it results in very little burden."

- Hebrews 4:15–16: "For we do not have a high priest who is unable to sympathize with our weaknesses, but one who in every respect has been tempted as we are, yet without sin. Let us then with confidence draw near to the throne of grace, that we may receive mercy and find grace to help in time of need." He is telling us to come to Him in boldness and certainty. If we ask for help, He will answer. He understands and has experienced suffering, so He can surely enter into the pain alongside us.

Whatever you are mourning in your life today—whether spiritual, emotional, or financial—He will be your comfort.

- Matthew 5:4: "Blessed are those who mourn, for they shall be comforted." This one particularly soothed my heart. God understands where I am today. He gave up His only Son for me. He understands my grief. He knows what it feels like to lose a child. Whatever you are mourning in your life today—whether spiritual, emotional, or financial—He will be your comfort. It is a promise to you.

- 1 Peter 5:7: "[Cast] all your anxieties on him, because he cares for you." It is so easy to choose worry over peace. God tells us to give our burdens to Him. He is surely able to care for them. If it is true that worry is a form of pride, then perhaps forgiveness is in order. Worry means, "I think I can fix or handle my circumstance on my own." Handing the burden over to Him confirms that I trust Him with it. This was one of the most difficult Scriptures for me, as worry had me enveloped. I was worried about my husband, my other two children, the grandparents, and Ramsey's little three-year-old classmates. So many questions and few answers.
- Psalm 42:5–6: "Why are you cast down, O my soul, and why are you in turmoil within me? Hope in God; for I shall again praise him, my salvation and my God."

I took comfort in the Scriptures. I needed His light. Meanwhile, I battled my own darkness.

Cynthia Swindoll describes depression as: "black as a thousand midnights in a cypress swamp. Loneliness that is indescribable. Confusion regarding God. Frustration with life and circumstances. The feeling that you have been abandoned, that you are worthless. Unlovable. The pain is excruciating."[14]

In her lowest points, she felt lonely, confused, frustrated,

---

14 Cynthia Swindoll quoted in Don Baker, *Depression: Finding Hope & Meaning in Life's Darkest Shadow* (Portland, OR: Multnomah, 1983), 5.

worthless, and unlovable. It is difficult to function with all these emotions facing you, constantly. I was there, too, and I chose to believe Psalm 30:5: "Weeping may tarry for the night, but joy comes with the morning." I placed my hope in Him when I could not see to take the next step. I was groping for light in the darkest of hours . . . and He reached for my hand.

I remember convincing myself that morning would never come. The pain was so deep and dark and my hope, gone. But just as He promises, morning does come. The dawn is on the horizon. Hold tight—the light is peeking through the window.

These particular verses were my life sources, my hope rope. They were promises that proved to me that I was going to make it through another day and that He would carry me through the valley if I would allow Him. I completely surrendered. I knew without Him, there was no way I was going to make it. He would be my strength, indeed! After a while, I chose to trust His promises.

COUCH BOUND

At the age of thirty-five, as a stay-at-home mom of three, I was in severe pain that could not be controlled with over-the-counter pain relief. Despite my age, my body felt more like a seventy-five-year-old's. I made an appointment with my physician and the tests began.

I spent the next two years being tested for various diseases. My white cell count was high. Inflammation indicators were high. Sedimentation rate was high. I had intermittent fever with bone pain that worsened with any form of exercise. I had continuous headaches that led to vomiting. Hip pain and back pain were almost unbearable. What in the world was wrong?

The initial diagnosis was osteoarthritis. I was medicated over the next six months with little or no improvement, and I endured multiple medication changes. As a result, the testing continued for various forms of multiple sclerosis, rheumatoid arthritis, systemic lupus erythematosus, Crohn's Disease, and various genetic autoimmune diseases. There were many appointments with neurologists, followed by tests for balance, physical response to touch, as well as nerve conduction velocity tests. I began to lose all hope.

After many, many months of excruciating pain and probing, a diagnosis was made: ankylosing spondylitis, or AS. According to the Spondylitis Association of America, this form of rheumatoid arthritis:

> primarily affects the spine, although other joints can become involved. It causes inflammation of the spinal joints (vertebrae) that can lead to severe, chronic pain and discomfort. In the most advanced cases (but not all cases), this inflammation can lead to new bone formation on the spine, causing the spine to fuse in a fixed, immobile position, sometimes creating a

forward-stooped posture. This forward curvature, or hunch of the spine, is called kyphosis . . . AS can also cause inflammation, pain, and stiffness in other areas of the body such as the shoulders, hips, ribs, heels and small joints of the hands and feet. Sometimes the eyes can become involved . . . The hallmark feature of ankylosing spondylitis is the involvement of the sacro-iliac (SI) joints during the progression of the disease, which are the joints at the base of the spine, where the spine joins the pelvis.[15]

It is permanent. It is painful. And it can be fatal.

The pain so was severe I could feel my hair and nails growing. Every part of my body ached continuously without any relief in sight. All the latest arthritis medications I had tried over the previous two years worked no more than a baby aspirin to the pain. It was not until the physician decided to try one of the original arthritis drugs, Indomethacin, that I found relief. There were horrible side effects to this dated medication, though: severe weight gain, headaches, dizziness, vomiting, swelling of the ankles and lower legs, increased heartbeat, excessive tiredness, lack of energy, severe flu-like symptoms, and confusion. I gained over one hundred pounds as a result of these various medications.

As my hips began to fuse, causing great difficulty in walking, I could make it down the stairs in the morning

---

15 "About Ankylosing Spondylitis," *Spondylitis Association of America,* http://www.spondylitis.org/about/as.aspx.

only to return in the evening for bed. I was unable to climb stairs. I was unable to walk for any distance. Driving became almost impossible, as I could not get out of the car once I reached my destination.

Jay began to drive the children to school, drive himself to the office (which was about twenty minutes away from our home), pick the children up after school, drive himself back to the office, and then home after work. Many days he had to prepare dinner when he arrived home in the evening. It was one of the most difficult times I can recall.

Jay resigned himself to the fact that he would need to get care for me at home soon. He was helping bathe me and dress me. He was my primary caregiver on top of all he did for the children and his veterinary practice.

During this period, especially after my diagnosis, I spent a lot of time with my children at home. I was unable to do much else, so this time was quality and quantity. Ramsey, then a rambunctious three-year-old, would lie on the sofa with me in the evenings and take a nap. He would bring toys to me, and we would play from the sofa. He was the legs I was unable to use at that time. As a toddler, he was fairly easy to entertain from the sofa. I basically became like a playmate to him.

I still recall one afternoon when I was having a good day. I drove myself to the school to pick him up. We passed a fast-food restaurant on the way home, which had just recently built an outside playground. He wanted to stop and play, and I simply could not do it. I knew it was all I could do to get him out of the car seat and into the house. He was so sad we couldn't play at the playground that day, so Jay took him the following day.

I struggled with day-to-day mobility prior to Ramsey's drowning. Now the pain in my heart only accentuated the pain in my body. I began to focus more on every detail of what I could not do, rather than what I could, and soon found myself hopeless.

I could hardly walk; most days I was unable to drive. I could not properly care for my boys, and now my heart was completely shredded. Oh, how the depression surrounded me.

HE SAID, "RUN!"

One Sunday morning in the summer of 2000, only two months after Ramsey's drowning, my pastor announced an upcoming mission trip into Zamora, Mexico, for twelve days. I remember sitting there hearing all the details and being so broken in my spirit—I felt like I was supposed to go, but how? That was impossible. I was not in a wheelchair yet, but it took everything within me just to get showered, get clothed, and make it to church. I often used a cane but tried not to use it in front of the children.

We got home after church, and with tear-filled eyes, my husband said, "Honey, you are supposed to go on the mission trip to Mexico." I started to cry. I remember sensing in my spirit while we sat in church that I was to go. I looked at Jay, and through uncontrollable tears, I reminded him of all the reasons that I could not go. I was unable to walk. I was unable to care for myself. How would I walk through the airport and take care of my luggage? He knew all this. Why would he suggest that I take this trip? He responded, "You have to go." I knew it, but why would God require this of me? I had nothing to give to anyone. Then I heard the Lord speak very softly to me: "Go and get healed."

I went to the first meeting on a Sunday evening and gathered all the information as we began to prepare for the trip. It would take place at the end of October, just five months after we buried our son.

A man named James desperately wanted to go on this trip but was struggling to get his funds together in time. My husband heard about his need and gave him a contribution. He later asked James to help get me through the airport, and he agreed. We packed the luggage, made it to the airport and through security, and onto the plane headed to Zamora, Mexico.

Then I heard the Lord speak very softly to me: "Go and get healed."

Oh, those children with big brown eyes. They looked so much like my little Ramsey. The boys especially would run to me and wrap their arms around my legs and hold tight, just as Ramsey used to do. I would stand there weeping and hugging these little ones. I was able to walk, but the pain was excruciating. Still, God was healing this mother's heart a little at a time.

We had been ministering in Mexico for several days, and on this particular day, we began our morning at the house of a local pastor. When we walked in it was set up for church; there were multiple white plastic chairs all in a row on a dirt floor, which was their living room. They had no roof. As we entered their modest home, the wife was still preparing for our arrival. With a homemade broom she busily swept the dirt floor where we would sit. The joy of the Lord surrounded this precious one. I remember hearing her humming as we entered their home. She was so happy to show us the different rooms. There were only two: the main living area and kitchen were combined, and there was a small room tucked away with a bed. The bed had no mattress. Still, she was so proud to show us her home. I have never felt so welcome as I did that day. All twelve of us sat down in Rubbermaid-type chairs on dirt floors and waited for our initial assignment. I spoke very little Spanish, but at least there were translators. Today our translator was a man from the church where we were ministering for the day.

During this twelve-day mission, our primary focus was to reach the children through music, skits, and puppets. We had also scheduled a crusade and would minister in multiple churches and Indian villages.

The pastor came out and said he wanted to bless our team of missionaries. One by one he called each person forward. I remember fretting over the fact that each person was being called to the front to be prayed for. How would I be able to walk to the front? He had no idea that I struggled to walk, because when he entered the room, we were already seated.

The translator would randomly point at a team member,

and they would walk forward toward them. He got to number eleven and I remember a sick feeling coming over me. I began to quietly weep. He had prayed over every one of our team members and never called me forward. He had surely forgotten me, the most broken woman in the world, in desperate need of a word from the Lord.

The pastor and translator stood talking while the other members of our team sat, quietly pondering the words that had just been adequately prophesied over them. I continued to quietly weep. I did not know many on my team, although we attended the same church. I am sure they could see my physical struggle, and they all knew about Ramsey's drowning.

All of a sudden the translator pointed to me. He did not know of my difficulties either, as this was the first time we had met him. The two of them began to walk toward me. They did not ask me to come forward. The pastor placed his hand upon me and began to weep. The pastor spoke zero English and used the translator the entire time. He wept and wept and wept as he stood over me, quietly praying and weeping.

I remember the all-encompassing heat that ran through my entire body as he prayed for me! I became weak in my extremities. By now, the whole team was crying. *What just happened to me?* I had never felt anything like it. It was overwhelming fire and weakness released throughout my body. This weakness that I was experiencing can only be described as lightness. Where I was previously aware of all the pain in my body, I was experiencing none of that! I was not afraid but startled by the feeling. I remember the feeling of fire but

bomb pops®, blow dryers, & butterfly kisses

my body was not perspiring. It was almost as if it ran through my veins. What was this? Honestly, I can't say that I was aware of a miracle happening because I didn't even know what that really meant. I just knew that *something* had happened to me at that very moment.

That night we arrived at the crusade. The evangelist was from Texas, and none of us knew him. It was the first time since our arrival that we did not need a translator.

The twelve of us were seated on the front row of the church. It was totally open without a roof and filled with people. I have never had such a feeling during worship. I could open my eyes and literally see the stars that He created twinkling just above my head. About a hundred voices were being lifted toward heaven in Spanish with random sounds of English, all singing simultaneously.

As worship ended and we sat down, the evangelist was introduced. I leaned over to grab my Bible, notepad, and pen from my purse when he began speaking. I heard him say, "Angel." Again, "Angel." The third time, "Angel."

James was sitting next to me and he leaned over, tapped me on the shoulder, and said, "Angelia . . . oh my, he is talking to you." I looked up and the evangelist was looking straight into my eyes.

In a loud voice he said, "Sister, you need to be running!" What? I was unable to walk without severe pain. Why was this man telling me to run? He said, "No! You need to get up right *now* and start running. Right now. Do it!"

I did not question his statement because he spoke with

— 76 —

such authority. He knew something that I did not yet know. I literally stood up from my seat and started running across the front of the church on the concrete slab floor. Running! Me! The woman who had struggled to walk just minutes before. I didn't feel any different. I didn't *feel* healed. But, you know what I did? I got up and I started running!

USED FOR GOOD

Suddenly, I understood the reason the Lord prompted my husband's heart as well as mine in the urgency of this trip. He never planned for me to minister to others while I was there, although I surely had many opportunities. He planned to heal me physically!

I was now able to see how the fatal disease was used for my good. Even with the pain, I celebrate the period of time I was home with Ramsey, as I was unable to do anything other than be there with him. I spent about eighteen months with Ramsey in close quarters as a result of my illness. It certainly slowed me down, so I could enjoy every moment with him. I experienced a lifetime of priceless memories and love and cuddles that otherwise I would have missed. In one moment I could look at all the pain and suffering and be so thankful for the journey.

Remember, this was in 2000. There were no cell phones and it was almost impossible to get a line through to the US. I talked to Jay twice on that trip; each time I basically had five minutes to tell him I had been healed and I was running. He wept like a child on the phone and said, "I knew God told me you were supposed to go and be healed." God had told me too. We just had no idea that meant *healed!*

It was confirmation that He was not only near and aware, but that He was actively moving.

When I arrived home, I *ran* through the airport to meet my family. My husband wept as he watched me with our children, each one staring in disbelief. They had not seen me this active and mobile in many years. We were all so broken, but we were experiencing the hand of God in very real way.

It was our first family encounter with the miraculous. Once you experience the miraculous, you are constantly in search of it again. He allowed us to be touched in a way that would catapult our journey to healing. It was confirmation that He was not only near and aware, but that He was actively moving. He showed us that He was El Roi, the God who sees us; and we met our healer, Jehovah-Rophe, face-to-face.

"I WILL NEVER BE BACK!"

My husband kept encouraging me to return to the rheumatologist for confirmation of my healing after my mission trip. I have to admit there was a little fear within me concerning this. I knew I had been healed, and I did not want anyone questioning it. It was still so new to me and I was not exactly sure how to handle it. Honestly, my heart did not want to go back into his office again and witness all those wheelchairs, broken countenances, and walkers. Could I not just continue forward, experiencing the healing of the Lord?

Jay explained to me that the people in the waiting room needed to be given some hope. He felt the physician needed some as well. So I made the appointment, reluctantly. When I showed up in the office, the women behind the counter could not believe what they were seeing. They wanted every detail of the experience, and I gladly shared it all! It really was a glorious moment, being able to bring hope into the room where there had previously been little to experience.

I told them how I had learned to live with the pain so I didn't even notice when it was gone, initially. I was so medicated and so broken during that mission trip. My focus was on those who were hurting and hungry—the little children gazing into my eyes looking for help and hope. Honestly, I wasn't even thinking about me. I knew I felt heat running through my body while I sat in the kind pastor's humble home in Mexico with the rest of my church group, as he prayed and cried over me. But it wasn't until the evangelist prophesied over me and said to get up and run that I realized I had been healed! The pain was gone. Completely gone. Never to return. That night I slept better than I had in years.

Next I sat in the exam room waiting for the physician. He walked through the door and his mouth dropped open. He was an unbeliever in the healing power of God and could not understand what he was witnessing. He began to weep. I began to weep. Then I shared the Gospel with him, describing the power of God Almighty! It was truly a beautiful experience, and I knew that I had done the right thing by coming.

I needed the X-rays to confirm my hips were no longer fused, although I knew it—I could feel it! There was confidence in claiming the work of God after having the X-rays in my hand.

As I rounded the corner to leave, the lady at the front desk looked and said, "When shall I schedule your next appointment?" With a skip in my step and a huge smile on my face, I replied, "I will never be back!"

chapter six

Slowly but Surely

My body was healed but my heart was still so broken. I continued to be tormented by people's comments from the night of the wake.

Many people asked me if we would be moving. First of all, I could not believe that people could be so insensitive at such a time as this. Why on earth would we consider a move? After all, so many memories were tied to that house in Madison, Alabama. Ramsey was a newborn when we purchased the home. He took his first step, spoke his first word, threw a ball, planted a flower, all at that house. We'd had all his Christmases at that house. Moving away was the last thing on my mind. I was unable to even entertain such a thought and honestly, was offended that anyone would suggest it.

It was a very trying year for our family. Both children were constantly being asked questions about their little brother's drowning. When we attended school functions we were often quizzed on the details. Every day was a day we had to be intentional about surviving.

Benjamin was simply going through the motions of life. Chandler was struggling with school. His teacher attempted to make his assignments of utmost importance, but honestly, Chandler was not impressed with her urgency. As a result, Jay had multiple meetings with her, trying to explain where we stood as a family, and the reason Chandler was responding in such a way. He had just observed death up close, and everything else paled in importance. If it did not pertain to the magnitude of the death of a family member, she probably was going to lose the battle. Schoolwork was insignificant to him. We made it through the school year but with not much success.

Several months into the next school year, Benjamin—now thirteen and about to start the ninth grade—began speaking with us about transferring to a local, private high school. He was quite athletic and their baseball program was outstanding, as well as their academic curriculum. I made the appropriate calls to find out there were no openings. We were okay with that, as the move to this school would require a physical move in order for him to be eligible for the upcoming baseball season.

Two weeks later the telephone call came. They had a place for our son in their program and asked us to move into the appropriate school district right away.

We began looking at apartment complexes within their district. The rules mandated our family live in that particular city at the time of application. Following a specific period of time, since it was a private institution, we would be allowed to live anywhere and drive into the school daily. We decided we would meet the requirement, then move back into our home after the nine-month period.

We moved into an apartment and made the decision to homeschool Chandler. We hoped healing would take place if we isolated him from the pressure of public school. I was trying to protect Chandler from all the questions. Jay and I just felt he needed one-on-one time in order to bring his world back to something a bit more normal, and we had hopes that his fears would subside.

We settled in very quickly. Benjamin began school in the second semester of his ninth-grade year, and Chandler's homeschooling began.

LAUGHTER AT LAST

After a couple of months my husband and I had a revelation almost simultaneously. He looked at me and said, "Honey, I am so sorry. I did not realize that the memories of the tragedy in that home was killing our family!" He was right. Every step we took reminded us of something about Ramsey. Every meal we prepared, every movie we watched—even the cat reminded us of something Ramsey did or said. Even though some of it was funny, the realization of him being gone was so overwhelming that a flood of sadness would wash over us. Now in the apartment, things began to change for the better.

I still remember hearing our family laugh for the first time in months. We were all tucked away safely in that little apartment watching a movie together. Our healing as a family had begun, but what about the house? The pain was too deep to simply walk away from our memories there. We agreed that we could never place a "For Sale" sign in the yard, but that if God supernaturally brought a buyer, we would sell it. Three weeks later, we had our answer.

It was a Wednesday morning, Jay's off day, and we left the apartment and headed to the house to mow the lawn. I agreed to go with him so we could get it done more quickly. I was on the riding mower and Jay was edging when a man walked over to me from the church parking lot next door.

I turned the mower off and he said, "Hi! I am the pastor next door. We want to buy your home." As he spoke, I looked up and saw Jay making his way over to us. I began to weep, then walked away as Jay continued the conversation with the pastor. We finished up the yard work without ever mentioning one word of what the man had just inquired.

We were seeing God move in a mighty way concerning our home. There was so much pain in keeping it, but almost more pain in releasing it. How would we ever be able to make the decision? We called the church the next day and told them we would pray about it. They agreed to do the same.

Several weeks passed before Jay called the pastor. The leadership from the church had met the week prior and prayed over the details. They came up with a price that they felt was fair, as they did not desire to haggle over the price of our home. They understood the difficulty of this decision for us. We prayed as well and when we met with their leadership concerning the sale, the amount that the Lord had given us for an asking price was exactly the amount they had agreed upon. I had only one request—that they cover the backyard pool with dirt. They agreed.

NEW BEGINNINGS

Several weeks later, with tears streaming down our cheeks, Jay and I signed the papers and sold our home. The move was quite emotional, as we had not touched Ramsey's room since his passing. His swords, his sandals, his clothes, and his favorite stuffed animals all lay in the floor next to his bed, behind closed doors, at the request of our other two children. The pain of walking by Ramsey's room several times throughout the day made life almost impossible. Chandler closed Ramsey's bedroom door, and we allowed it to remain closed.

My oldest sister and her husband came over one afternoon and agreed to pack up Ramsey's room for us. It was one of those things I could not face. After all, what were we supposed to do with Ramsey's things? They very carefully packed away all those precious memories, keeping in a trunk the items that we could not part with, even briefly. Today, those remain in that same wicker trunk in our home, since there wasn't a bedroom for Ramsey.

We realize that no matter where we go or what we do Ramsey will always be in our hearts.

For our family, the physical move was the beginning of our healing. Although our hearts were breaking into pieces, it would be this physical move that would begin the journey. The memories are still with us. We realize that no matter where we go or what we do Ramsey will always be in our hearts. Picking up and packing up was so difficult but so necessary for our family.

THE KEY OF "F" AND FRIENDSHIP

The Bible declares that worship is a physical act as well as an intelligent and spiritual one (Romans 12:1). Throughout the Scriptures we find many physical signs of worship:

1. Kneeling before the Lord—submission, obedience, devotion (Psalm 95:6)
2. Lifting your hands to God as your source—adoration, thankfulness, surrender (Psalm 134:2)
3. Standing in awe before your King—honor (Psalm 22:23)
4. Clapping your hands with rejoicing—celebration (Psalm 47:1)
5. Dancing in praise—joy (Psalm 149:3)
6. Bowing your head—humility (Exodus 12:27)
7. Shouting before the Lord—celebration (Psalm 33:1)

8. Prostrating yourself—dependency (Job 1:20)
9. Making music—playing instruments
   (Revelation 15:2)
10. Singing—making melody with your heart
    (Ephesians 5:19)

One particular afternoon, I was at the school fields waiting for Benjamin's baseball game to begin. It was the first game of the season after Ramsey's passing. Chandler was playing with friends, and I sat alone in the stands waiting for the first pitch. Leisa, a woman I had met several times at games the previous year, walked up and sat beside me. Her son played on the same baseball team as Benjamin, and her younger son had played at the park with Chandler and Ramsey during the games. We could watch the children and watch the game, simultaneously. This was the first time I had seen her since Ramey's drowning. Did she know? Had she heard?

She simply leaned over and hugged me. She sat and listened as I poured out my brokenness, and not once did she give me any instruction, advice, or input. She simply listened, loved, cried, and comforted as best she could.

As we sat and chatted, she mentioned that she had a CD she needed me to listen to. She said, "I believe it will be a blessing to you." She called her husband, Rusty, and asked him to bring it to the field after his meeting. Rusty and Leisa co-pastor a church in the neighboring city. Little did I know that my healing was about to take another step forward because of their obedience to deliver a worship CD. It was Rita Springer's latest. I had never heard of this worship leader, but God used her to take my healing to the next level.

GIRL TALK

Soon after our true friendship began, Leisa invited me to the upcoming women's conference at her church. It would take place during early September. This three-day conference turned out to be on Ramsey's birthday—his first birthday after the drowning. She told me that Rita Springer would be leading worship, and she really believed I needed to come.

I had not been getting out much. I even bought groceries miles from home to avoid people. I felt the whole world knew of my circumstance, and the constant gawking from others was more than I could bear. I did not think I could go to the conference, but I kept hearing her voice: "I really believe you need to be there. You need to be in the middle of this worship." I prayed, got my clothes on, and through many tears, I showed up for the conference.

As I stood in the foyer during a brief period prior to the start of the meeting, I second-guessed my presence in the midst of all these women who appeared to be celebrating. I contemplated making a run for it. All of a sudden, I looked to my left and I saw Leisa coming toward me. She was so happy to see me. She walked right up and wrapped her arms around me. She said, "I am so glad you could come!" This huge smile came across her face, and I knew I was supposed to be there. That moment would begin a lifelong friendship.

I walked into the sanctuary and the worship began. I will never forget the feeling within me as the voices were being lifted to God. There were several hundred women all in worship, all with stories, all placing their burdens aside and focusing on the holiness of God. I recall sliding into the floor, flat on my face, thanking Him for helping me arrive at that place. Yes, I realized that because of His strength I was at that conference in the presence of Him. It was exactly where I needed to be that day. Nobody even noticed that I was wailing in the floor on my face. There were many others alongside me.

Rita Springer began to share the story behind one of her songs. It was called "Fragrant Offering" and was about a woman who had buried her little daughter. The mother had some very expensive perfume that had been given to her by her husband. The little girl, Caroline, wanted to wear some, and she accidentally dropped the entire bottle in her parents' carpeted powder room. Half the bottle was lost. About six months after the little girl was buried, her mother dropped an earring in the floor and bent down to pick it up, and when she did . . . the fragrance of the perfume that had been spilled filled her nostrils. She fell to her knees weeping.

Several months later the mother sent a letter to the perfume designer about her story. He mailed her a gorgeous crystal container that held one gallon of this costly perfume! He also gave her a lifelong supply.

"Fragrant Offering"*
by Rita Springer

I bring to you a fragrant offering
I pour out my life and I wash your feet
I offer up to you oh Lord this brokenness
What you can see in me shall be my confidence

May it be a pleasing fragrance
That I bring to you oh my Lord
I am so in need of your presence
That I bow before you now
I pour my vial of worship over you (x2)

I bring to you a humble sacrifice
I pour out my heart and I give you my life
I offer up to you oh Lord this costly gift
And with absolute abandon now
My love I confess

When the first word of her song came off her lips, I thought I would not be able to breathe. She had tapped into

---

my pain and was speaking straight into my spirit. I knew I was supposed to be there that weekend. She had shared another mother's tragedy, and the words she delivered broke me even further; but the song changed my path. The line that stuck in my head over the next twelve months was, "I offer up to you, oh Lord, this brokenness. I am in need of your presence." Sweet and simple. I know this song was originally written for someone else, but what I realized was that the same brokenness Rita describes here is my brokenness as well. There is a familiar crushing that results from the loss of a child. This familiarity is one I never dreamed I would experience.

Two weeks later, my husband and I felt the Lord was releasing us to serve in the church where Rusty and Leisa co-pastor. We had served faithfully for years in our previous church, but we now felt the Lord was allowing us to fill a niche in this new home and that He would take us to another level of healing.

We met with the pastors and explained the move we felt led to make. The Lord would use this move to catapult our healing in motion; and for me, the greatest impact came through the introduction to Rita Springer's worship and the friendship of Leisa Nelson. It was through Rita's personal struggles, her suffering, and her ability to pen lyrics that God would strengthen her spirit as well as mine. It was through Leisa's ability to love like Jesus that I was able to grieve in a safe place.

Rita released another song that brought hope to this mother's heart. When isolation seemed to take my breath

I am amazed at the tools God will use to minister to His children when they are suffering through the blows of this fallen world.

away, I could hear Rita's voice: "I have to believe that He sees my darkness. I have to deny that I am alone." I can remember lying in the floor and singing these lyrics along with her, just weeping from the depths of my soul. Her song "I Choose to Believe" became my anthem even when I didn't feel I could believe.

I am amazed at the tools God will use to minister to His children when they are suffering through the blows of this fallen world. He knows exactly what will penetrate each of our hearts to bring about healing, and He is faithful to provide it. For me, it was worship! It was a trusting friendship that would listen without judgment and love me through it, unconditionally.

chapter seven

I'm Gonna Need to See
That in Writing!

I never questioned God's love. I loved Him completely. But it was time to take our relationship to another level. What I understood previously was not enough to hold me as I faced the drowning of my youngest son. I began to question myself. Did I really know Him at all?

I had experienced firsthand what it meant to hold my last breath in the palm of His hand (Job 12:10). I realized in the midst of suffering that I had to have some answers. I was hearing things from people "all in the name of the Lord" that crushed my spirit, things that did not line up with what I understood to be fact. I could no longer stand on what I had been told nor what I heard over the years.

I remember the day in 2006 when I felt the Lord nudging me to seminary. I had ignored these nudges over the past couple of years during my personal studies because I had formed my own idea of what seminary was, and I wasn't at all interested. I begged Him not to make me go. But that particular day in prayer, I felt His words come into my spirit, saying, "If you do not do it now, you will be in disobedience."

Through many tears, I made an appointment with my senior pastor. My husband supported me 100 percent, and together we went in to meet with the pastor about the next step. Now, my husband had seen this call on my life for years. As a matter of fact, he had pushed me to attend seminary many, many years before, and I would have nothing to do with it then either. I was full of fire and excitement, enthusiasm and joy, and I didn't want any part of anything that was less enthusiastic than I was about the mission.

So there we sat in Pastor Rusty's office asking him whether I should go to seminary. He looked into my eyes and said, "Absolutely. I was wondering when you would take that step." I literally cried myself into a puddle. Next, I met with one of my spiritual mentors for confirmation. He immediately directed me to Jack Hayford's seminary, The King's University, in Van Nuys, California. It was there my academic training would begin, and also where my heart would begin another level of mending.

In search of deeper truths, I wanted to grab hold of an infinite God with my finite mind.

In search of deeper truths, I wanted to grab hold of an infinite God with my finite mind. I was encouraged by professors to pray as painful topics were uncovered, to meditate on the teachings, and to allow the Holy Spirit to bring it alive, releasing clarity. They knew my story and they understood the sensitivity of the time. They also knew I'd have a lot of questions.

There were terms used on a regular basis that felt uncomfortable to me. One was the word *meditate*, which they explained is often misunderstood. The clearest definition that I have read comes from Dr. J. I. Packer. He defines meditation upon the Word as: "the activity of calling to mind, and thinking over, and dwelling on, and applying to oneself, the various things that one knows about the works and ways and purposes and promises of God. It is an activity of holy thought, consciously performed in the presence of God, under the eye of God, by the help of God, as a means of communion with God."[16] After that explanation, I got it! The Holy Spirit reveals to us the deep things of God (1 Corinthians 2:10–12) and the mystery of Christ (Ephesians 3:3–5).

I was also struggling with the reading of the Word. I would read it and not understand anything I had just read. I didn't know if it was because of the depression distracting me, or if I had just not yet tapped into the truth that it was written for me, to me, and somewhat about me. I knew I probably wasn't the only student struggling with this, but I was determined to work through it. I had to know more about God.

During this time, I was often reminded of how some describe the Word's impact upon them:

"As sweet as honey," according to Ezekiel 3:3;

---

16 J. I. Packer, *Knowing God* (Downers Grove, IL: InterVarsity Press, 1973), 18–19.

"a lamp to my feet and a light to my path," in Psalm
119:105;

"renewal of your mind," declares Romans 12:2;

"a burning fire shut up in my bones," from Jeremiah 20:9;

"more precious than gold" and "sweeter than honey,"
claims Psalm 19:10 (NIV);

"perfect," "refreshing, and "trustworthy," sings Psalms
19:7 (NIV); and a

"joy and the delight of my heart," celebrates Jeremiah
15:16.

I wanted His Word to be as sweet as honey and more
precious than gold to me. I wanted the experience that others
described. Although I felt hindered, there was a fire burning
in my heart, as Jeremiah mentioned, that kept me pushing
for more. I had to know everything I could about who God
was. What is He like? How does He feel about me? How can
I *know* Him rather than just know *about* Him? Is this even
a possibility?

I felt these answers would address some of the questions
I carried about Ramsey's drowning. So, I began a study of
His character.

WHAT ARE HIS CHARACTER TRAITS?

According to Psalm 34:15, He is attentive to me.
He is available, declares Matthew 11:28–30.

He is good, says Psalm 136:1.

He is compassionate, states 1 John 3:17.

Dependable describes Him in Luke 16:10.

He is faithful according to Revelation 17:14.

He is forgiving in Psalm 130:4.

He is gentle in James 3:17.

He is love in 1 John 4:8.

He is sensitive in Romans 12:15.

He is mercy in Psalm 37:26.

He is truth in Proverbs 12:22.

These verses do not describe a God who means harm toward me. As a matter of fact, these are traits I desire to mirror. I want to be attentive, available, compassionate, and dependable in the eyes of those I encounter. Repeatedly reading these truths assured me that my understanding of the God I serve was on point. He loves me. He is kind toward me. He has plans to prosper me and not to harm me, according to Jeremiah 29:11.

As I continued to study God, I found common ground among most theologians in describing "how we can know Him." They suggest two methods: *General Revelation* and *Special Revelation*.

Professor John McKendricks from Multnomah University clearly explained the two:

1. *General Revelation* can include the cosmos (starry sky), the sunrise and sunset, the birth of a child,

or myriad other miraculous events that cause us to know there is a God.

I remember feeling certain that I could not survive the pain I was experiencing after burying Ramsey. I was convinced that no human could watch their son being pulled from the bottom of the pool and observe all the rescue workers' failed attempts at resuscitation and live to share the story. Suddenly, I realized it was a miracle I was even surviving. I was experiencing this general revelation firsthand.

2. *Special Revelation* is belief that the knowledge of God is discovered through supernatural means, like miracles and most importantly, the Scriptures. It is considered an imparted revelation or a disclosure of God's truth through divine means and intent, outside of man's ability to reason.

I have a very close relationship with my brother, Mike. He and Robin were going through a devastating divorce that he did not want, and we talked on the phone multiple times every day. He cried and I listened for what seemed like hours at a time. He was in so much pain, and I remember feeling completely helpless. All that I could do was pray for him, listen to him, and be there for him. There is nothing I would not have done to soften the blows he took. My heart was breaking. As much as I love Mike, which is with all my heart, God revealed to me that *He* "sticks closer than a brother" (Proverbs 18:24).

God also shows Himself to His creation through our experiences. For some, the experience of salvation lends tremendous knowledge of God as He reveals Himself as Savior.

During one of the darkest times of my life in the summer of 1987, I found myself sitting in the bedroom floor at twenty-five years old, crying out to a God I didn't have a relationship with. I could see no way out of my circumstance. I had made multiple decisions that had placed me where only God could help me. Desperation caused me to drop to my knees that day. Still, although I didn't yet know Him, He heard my cry and turned His face toward me. It was through this encounter that He placed an insatiable hunger to know Him and to dialogue with Him that continues to this day. This encounter with God—my salvation experience—laid the groundwork for my feet to remain steady for the journey that was ahead.

Experiencing the drowning of my son caused God to be revealed in a completely different way. There was an intimacy that occurred that day and would continue for the following eighteen months that has never been duplicated. His presence . . . continuous. His hand . . . obvious. His comfort . . . undeniable.

It was during this exposure that God was most recognizable to me in His creation. People from all walks of life suddenly looked like Him. He directed individuals to me with specific words that only He could have delivered. Only He knew the information they would utter. It was through this experience that the Love of God was most evident. Hearing

His voice become the clearest that I ever heard. I was confident that He was near. And not only near but that He had me surrounded with His care.

As I continued my search for more, I was introduced to two more terms that made a significant impact upon my understanding concerning God and His presence. I needed to know He was more than God Almighty. I needed to know He was near me and that He knew me.

The two words that captivated me were *transcendence* and *immanence*. According to Dr. Wayne Grudem, transcendence refers to how God is completely "other" than us, beyond us in His nature and character. He is not part of it. He made it and rules it but is independent of it. He defines immanence as referring to God's presence, closeness, and constant involvement in creation.

These two words pointed me to the truth that I was in search of. Yes, God created all things—He is transcendent—but He is also near me. He is in constant involvement with all things that concern me. He is immanent. He not only gives life but He is in relationship with all He has created.

Think about the ideas of transcendence and immanence in relation to how God reveals Himself to us: general revelation and special revelation. General revelation is given to all people, at all times, and in all places, declaring something of God's greatness. However, God's personal traits, His grace, His goodness, and His faithfulness, cannot usually be known through general revelation. For that, we need special revelation through supernatural means.

ATTRIBUTES OF GOD

What are attributes? They are the characteristics of the nature of God. Attributes are not the acts He performs, such as creating and guiding. We are asking, "What is He like?"

Attributes are qualities of the Triune Godhead: Father, Son, and Holy Spirit. These are permanent qualities. They cannot be lost or gained. They are inseparable from the being or essence of God. To better attempt to understand God, various systems of classifying His attributes are available to us. There are clearly two types defined by theologians, and I choose to use the model set by Dr. Stanley J. Grenz:[17]

I. The Absolute (Incommunicable) Greatness Attributes: How Is God Different from Us?

1. Spirituality

He is spirit; He is not composed of matter, nor does he possess a physical nature. John 4:24 declares, "God is spirit."

In 1 Timothy 1:17, we see Him described as "the King of ages, immortal, invisible, the only God."

So, God is spirit. He is invisible. He has no body and therefore, no limitation.

---

17 Stanley J. Grenz, *Theology for the Community of God* (Grand Rapids: Eerdmans, 2000), 90. The model consisting of the nine attributes is Dr. Grenz's, but the anecdotal stories and scripture added throughout the rest of this chapter are by the author.

2. Life

He is alive. This characteristic of God is prominent in the contrast frequently drawn between Him and other gods. He is the living God as contrasted with inanimate objects of metal or stone.

Isaiah 46:5–7: "To whom will you liken me and make me equal, and compare me, that we may be alike? Those who lavish gold from the purse, and weigh out silver in the scales, hire a goldsmith, and he makes it into a god; then they fall down and worship! They lift it to their shoulders, they carry it, they set it in its place, and it stands there; it cannot move from its place. If one cries to it, it does not answer or save him from his trouble."

If a god has to be carried, how can it unburden its worshipers? If a god cannot move, how can it intervene on anyone's behalf? The greatest revelation I received here is that other gods must be carried; but my God wants to carry me.

3. Personality

He is spiritual, alive, and personal. He is capable of feeling, choosing, and having a reciprocal relationship with other personal and social beings.

It is evident in Scripture that God has personality. Consider that God has a name. He has a name, which He assigns to Himself and by which He reveals himself.

In biblical times names were not merely labels to distinguish one person from another as they are today. The

Hebrew approach was different. A name was chosen very carefully and with attention to its significance.

When Moses wonders how he should respond when the Israelites ask for the name of who has sent him, God identifies Himself as "I am" or "I will be": Yahweh, Jehovah, the Lord (Exodus 3:14). Here God's name reflects His eternity; that He is the "continually existing *One*, declaring . . . I will be with you!"

God has a personality. He has a name just like you and I do. Can you imagine having a best friend but you didn't even know their name? That's hardly a friend at all if you haven't even exchanged names. He wants to be relational with us. He knows *your* name (Psalm 91:14).

4. Self-existence

God is the absolute source of all life and being, the uncaused, the Cause. He is not one in a series. He is the eternal, living God, Creator of all things and all things that have ever existed. "And he is before all things, and in him all things hold together" (Colossians 1:17). God is not dependent for "being" upon any source outside Himself, making Him self-existent.

Theologian Wayne Grudem states that God's existence is evident throughout the Bible. The first verse of Genesis does not present evidence for the existence of God but immediately tells what He has done: "In the beginning, God created the heavens and the earth."

If we are convinced that the Bible is true, then we know

from the Word not only that God exists but also very much about His nature and His acts. Through studying and meditating on the Scriptures, God reveals Himself to creation. His attributes come to life. His character becomes evident. His identity is undeniable.

5. Immutability (unchangeableness)

God does not change in His being, in His perfections, His purposes, and His promises; yet He does act and feel emotions, and He acts and feels differently in response to different situations. I appreciate this response found in the Westminster Shorter Catechism, "What is God?" The answer read as follows: "God is Spirit, infinite, eternal, and unchangeable, in his being, wisdom, power, holiness, justice, goodness, and truth." The great Charles Hodge described this statement as "probably the best definition of God ever penned by man."[18] "For I the Lord do not change" (Malachi 3:6).

"Every good gift and every perfect gift is from above, coming down from the Father of lights with whom there is no variation or shadow due to change" (James 1:17). There is nothing in this world that is truly good that has any origin other than from above!

Paul, more than anyone else, expresses the unchanging love of Christ in Romans 8:38–39: "For I am sure that neither death nor life, nor angels nor rulers, nor things present nor things to come, nor powers, nor height nor depth, nor

---

18 Charles Hodge, quoted in J. I. Packer, *Knowing God*, 21.

anything else in all creation, will be able
to separate us from the love of God in
Christ Jesus our Lord."

*There is nothing
that you can do to
cause Him to remove
His love for you.*

One of the first truths I learned about
God was that He *is* love. This was difficult for me. The truth is, I don't have
to prove myself, nor do I have to earn it
from Him. He simply loves me. He loves Ramsey. He loves
you. There is nothing that you can do to cause Him to remove
His love for you. He never changes.

6. Eternity

His existence is from everlasting past to everlasting future.
The Apostle John writes: "'I am the Alpha and the Omega,'
says the Lord God, 'who is and who was and who is to come,
the Almighty'" (Revelation 1:8). He is the beginning of all
history and the goal for whom all things are made.

Knowing that God is the beginning and the end and
everything in between lends confidence that He was there
before Ramsey's drowning, at Ramsey's drowning, and after
the drowning. The outcome, knowing that Ramsey's spirit
is in the presence of God, will not change because God is
eternal.

7. Omnipresent

God is everywhere, present. However, He is "in" some
specific places in manifestation: He met Moses at the burning bush and on the mount. He is in the temple, yet it can't

hold Him! He is in heaven, yet He fills heaven and earth. He is on His throne where Jesus intercedes at His right hand, yet He has promised, "I am with you always" (Matthew 28:20).

Omnipresent is defined as God being near or present to all things. It means that regardless of where you are currently—based on your past events, present events, or future events—He is there. This definition affirms how God's omnipresence is closely connected to our declaration that He is eternal as well.

In the Old Testament, God manifested Himself as Jehovah Shammah—"God is present." God was present as Lord in all creation, and there is no escaping Him. He is present in the innermost thoughts. Even as we are formed in the womb, He knows all the days of our future.

David expresses God's omnipresence best in Psalm 139:7–10:

> *Where shall I go from your Spirit?*
> *Or where shall I flee from your presence?*
> *If I ascend to heaven, you are there!*
> *If I make my bed in Sheol, you are there!*
> *If I take the wings of the morning*
> *and dwell in the uttermost parts of the sea,*
> *even there your hand shall lead me,*
> *and your right hand shall hold me.*

Nowhere in the entire universe can you flee from God's presence. This is where I began to receive some peace. I was tormented on a regular basis with the thought that my son had faced his greatest fear alone. I suddenly had a revelation during this study that Ramsey was not standing near the poolside alone. No! The very presence of God had Him surrounded. I have to believe because of the peace that this presence delivers that Ramsey, too, felt the arms of God.

He was there, at the pool. He is here, as I write. He is right there with you as you are reading this.

He was there, at the pool. He is here, as I write. He is right there with you as you are reading this. We should never feel that we are alone. The truth is, we never are.

8. Omniscience

Nothing happens anywhere that God is unaware of. Psalm 139:1–4 declares, "O Lord, you have searched me and known me! You know when I sit down and when I rise up; you discern my thoughts from afar. You search out my path and my lying down and are acquainted with all my ways. Even before a word is on my tongue, behold, O Lord, you know it altogether."

Let us take a look at the account of Ananias and Sapphira:

But a man named Ananias, with his wife Sapphira, sold a piece of property, and with his wife's knowledge he kept back for himself some of the proceeds and brought only a part of it and laid it at the apostles' feet. But Peter said, "Ananias, why has Satan filled your heart to lie to the Holy Spirit and to keep back for yourself part of the proceeds of the land? While it remained unsold, did it not remain your own? And after it was sold, was it not at your disposal? Why is it that you have contrived this deed in your heart? You have not lied to man but to God." When Ananias heard these words, he fell down and breathed his last. And great fear came upon all who heard of it. The young men rose and wrapped him up and carried him out and buried him. After an interval of about three hours his wife came in, not knowing what had happened. And Peter said to her, "Tell me whether you sold the land for so much." And she said, "Yes, for so much." But Peter said to her, "How is it that you have agreed together to test the Spirit of the Lord? Behold, the feet of those who have buried your husband are at the door, and they will carry you out." Immediately she fell down at his feet and breathed her last. When the young men came in they found her dead, and they carried her out and buried her beside her husband. And great fear came upon the whole church and upon all who heard of these things. (Acts 5:1–11)

He knows all things from the beginning. He knows the future, for He is the one who can say He is God, and there is none like Him, "declaring the end from the beginning and from ancient times things not yet done" (Isaiah 46:10).

Nothing surprises God. He knows our actions and our thoughts. He knows every detail about His creation.

According to Matthew 10:30, every hair on our head is numbered and He knows them. He knows our needs before they are spoken. All of God's knowledge is always fully present in His consciousness; it neither grows dim nor fades into nonconscious memory. His knowledge never changes or grows. He has known all things that would happen and all things that He would do prior to eternity.

THE INCIDENT

I remember referring to Ramsey's drowning as "the accident." I was unable to say the words *died* or *death* or *drowning*, so I used the phrase "the accident."

One day the Lord spoke very gently to my broken heart and said this: "It's okay to refer to the passing of Ramsey as 'the incident' but not 'the accident.' By using the term 'the accident' you are declaring that I was unaware of the moment and was caught off guard. I was there the whole time."

Not only did this open my eyes to the ever-present God, but it also demonstrated to me that He saw, He was aware, and He was near. I wept uncontrollably after sensing His voice. I was not crying that He corrected me—I was crying because He wanted me to know that He never left Ramsey's side. This revelation unveiled the love of God to me like I have never known.

God represents the purest form of love that exists. This love is not for the chosen few but is simply part of the ordinary Christian experience. He not only exhibits this holy love but according to 1 John 4:8, He is love. Even when it is impossible to sense His presence or the ability to see that He is aligning things on our behalf, there is confidence in knowing that love is in and behind all that is occurring. He is near!

9. Omnipotence

"Ah, Lord God! It is you who have made the heavens and the earth by your great power and by your outstretched arm! Nothing is too hard for you" (Jeremiah 32:17).

Omnipotent is a theological term that refers to the all-encompassing power of God. He is the all-powerful Lord who has created all things and sustains them by the Word of His power. He reveals in His Word that He is all-powerful and in the final analysis, He is the ruler of nature and history. In Genesis 17:1, God revealed himself to Abram as God Almighty, or El-Shaddai. This particular name was very rarely used and was reserved for describing the almighty power of God. His infinite power is also demonstrated in Scripture in connection with His creation. He spoke. He breathed. He actively created.

God's power is evident in His sovereign rule over all things. We see it demonstrated by His power in the church. He took twelve seemingly ordinary disciples, filled them with His Spirit, and with them "turned the world upside down"

(Acts 17:6). His power is evident in the resurrection of Jesus from the dead, demonstrating God's power over the realm of death and the grave. He is also sovereign over angels, principalities and powers, demon spirits, and Satan himself.

He who made all things and rules all realms can surely handle any problem that you and I are facing. Amen!

II. The Moral (Communicable) Goodness Attributes: How Is God Like Us?

There are moral attributes that He shares to a limited degree with those He has rescued. These pertain to conduct and character:

Goodness	Love
Mercy	Holiness
Grace	Peace (or Order)
Patience	Righteousness (or Justice)

Jesus came to bridge the tension that exists between humanity and Himself, as well as between all of humanity that resulted because of the decision that Adam and Eve made (Genesis 3). It is impossible for us to experience these attributes at the level that God intended without the help of the Holy Spirit.

Once salvation is chosen and the Holy Spirit fills us, then we are able to encounter these in their truest form. I am reminded of Galatians 5:22–23: "But the fruit of the Spirit is love, joy, peace, patience, kindness, goodness, faithfulness, gentleness, self-control." These are all results of the Holy Spirit residing within the believer and will become more evident as we submit our lives to His plan rather than our own. We love at a very shallow level without God in our lives. We only have the ability to be kind based on "our" understanding of what kindness is rather than on God's intention of kindness for us.

We love at a very shallow level without God in our lives.

God's whole being includes all of His attributes: He is entirely loving, entirely merciful, entirely just. This lends a fairly good description of the character traits of God that are easily understood by His creation. Perhaps we struggle to fully understand His greatness attributes with our finite and limited minds because He is an infinite God; but since we share His moral attributes we are better able to recognize a loving God with nothing but the best planned for us. We are familiar with these terms and should be able to recognize them in one another. These define a loving, caring, and forgiving God. It also helps us determine the greatness of God, leading to a healthy reverential fear of who He is. Again, we are able to see that He is *great* but He is also *intimate* with His creation.

We are given many individual names for God from the Bible, and all of them reflect some aspect of His character. These are given to assist us in better understanding the nature of God. In Isaiah He is described as a lion (31:4); in Deuteronomy, an eagle and a rock (32:11, 4); in Isaiah, a lamb

(53:7); in Psalms, a light, a hiding place, and a shield (27:1, 119:114, 84:11); and in Proverbs, a tower (18:10). These are all very powerful and comforting terms. We are able to recognize the stability, the protection, the gentleness, the comfort, and the strength that He is to us.

There are more names from the Bible that we are given to help us recognize Him at a more personal level. He is described as a bridegroom, husband, judge, and king in Isaiah (61:10, 54:5, 33:22). He is a father in Deuteronomy (32:6). He is a shepherd in the Psalms (23:1). He is a healer in Exodus (15:26). After studying these particular names, I was able to sense the more personal side of God toward me. For me, He is demonstrated in these particular terms as "I am." He is demonstrated here as whatever you need Him to be. According to Genesis 1:10, He is seeing. In Exodus, He is hearing (2:24). In Isaiah, He is wiping away tears (25:8). This describes not only a loving God but also one who is intimate in your suffering.

The reason I am sharing all these passages is to demonstrate that in one sense or another *all* of creation reveals something about God to us; and the higher creation, especially man who is made in His image, reveals it more fully! (This is general revelation.) The terms God chose from His Word to reveal Himself to us describe events, feelings, or circumstances common to our experiences are special revelation.

After much study, He has revealed Himself to me. He is near. He was there at that poolside. He knew it was going to

He knew you would be reading this book right now, and that I would be sharing with you just how much He loves, understands, and desires to be in relationship with you.

happen. He knew I would pen this book in an attempt to bring healing to myself as well as others. He knew you would be reading this book right now, and that I would be sharing with you just how much He loves, understands, and desires to be in relationship with you. He is El Roi, the God who sees you, right now!

chapter eight

What? No Wings! I Was Told There'd Be Wings.

One night as I was writing (and was about to delete this chapter), I got news that a friend of mine discovered her young son had passed away in his sleep. Just a few hours prior to this news, I explained to God in prayer that I did not want to include a chapter on death, heaven, hell, and dying in this book. Who wants to hear about all of that anyway?

Immediately after hearing the news of my friend's son, I realized these were the very questions that haunted *my* heart. I heard so much chatter, prayers, words, and promises after Ramsey passed—but I needed *evidence* of these truths! I knew that was the only way I would find peace. So, I dedicate this chapter to all those in desperate need of answers concerning their loved ones' whereabouts at *this very moment*.

I will address many of my own questions in this chapter as well as questions that others have asked me. After extensive research and years of study, I still do not consider myself an authority on this topic; so I consulted the works of theologians Dr. Wayne Grudem and Dr. Stanley Grenz, as well as Drs. Daniel Brown and Billy Graham.

FEAR OF THE UNKNOWN

As a young child, through early adulthood, and up until Ramsey passed, I had great fear of death. It was so foreign. So final, it seemed. And there were so many opinions . . . I didn't know what to believe.

After Ramsey's death, I heard accounts of people's understanding concerning heaven. The torment of all the questions and scenarios flooded my heart and mind.

Most said I should be celebrating in the confidence that Ramsey was in heaven. I didn't have any trouble accepting the fact that his spirit was in the presence of God, but where was that exactly?

People were describing white marshmallow-like clouds, family members with wings playing harps, and rainbows with unicorns—like heaven is one big Charmin commercial.

People were describing white marshmallow-like clouds, family members with wings playing harps, and rainbows with unicorns—like heaven is one big Charmin commercial. Those seem like comforting thoughts until you're actually faced with the desperate need to know where your beloved family member or friend went upon their death.

FALLOUT FROM THE FALL

According to the creation account in the Book of Genesis, God spoke into chaos and created order. He never intended for His creation to experience death, either physically or spiritually. However, death is introduced in Genesis 2:16–17: "And the Lord God commanded the man, saying, 'You may surely eat of every tree of the garden, but of the tree of the knowledge of good and evil you shall not eat, for in the day that you eat of it you shall surely die.'" The moment he ate of the fruit he died spiritually, separating himself from the fellowship of God, yet he lived for 930 years (Genesis 5:5).

As a result of disobedience, death entered in. This is better known as the "Fall of Man." Romans 5:12 confirms this: "Therefore, just as sin came into the world through one man, and death through sin, and so death spread to all men because all sinned." Death is the result of a fallen world, and we are all members of a fallen race. As Jack Hayford writes, "The residual fallout of the Fall continually appears around us in the form of sickness, sin, natural disaster, tragedy and death."[19]

I understood the reason we experience death and the ramifications that come with the process, still I continued to have questions. Namely, where was Ramsey at the moment life left his little body?

---

19 Jack Hayford, *I'll Hold You in Heaven* (Ventura, CA: Regal, 2003), 81–82.

According to Paul in 2 Corinthians 5:8, "Yes, we are of good courage, and we would rather be away from the body and at home with the Lord." Paul is saying that his physical body will be buried but his spirit will go immediately into the presence of God with no waiting room and no falling through total darkness. Paul's desire here became my desire also and I had the miraculous confidence that Ramsey was *immediately* in the presence of God.

INTO HIS PRESENCE

The state of the Christian, human body between death and resurrection is oftentimes referred to as "intermediate" or "present heaven."[20] This is not to be confused with our final destination coming at the time when Jesus returns and we receive our glorified bodies. I will address this later in the chapter. This is also not to be confused with what some refer to as purgatory. The idea of purgatory began in medieval times. Its purpose was to purify the dead of their sins.

Colossians declares, "And you, who were dead in your trespasses and the uncircumcision of your flesh, God made alive together with him, having forgiven us all our trespasses, by canceling the record of debt that stood against us with its legal demands. This he set aside, nailing it to

---

20 Randy Alcorn, *Heaven* (Carol Stream, IL: Tyndale, 2004), 59.

the cross. He disarmed the rulers and authorities and put them to open shame, by triumphing over them in him" (2:13–15). Christ's death and resurrection purchased our salvation, wholly. If purgatory were true, it would cheapen the work of Jesus on the cross.

The fact that the souls of believers go immediately into the presence of God confirms that there is no need for such a place as purgatory, limbo, or oblivion, and there is surely no reason for delay before coming into His presence. Jesus already paved the way. We are in His presence the moment we take the last breath, and we are immediately in the "present heaven" awaiting Jesus' return to earth for His church.

WILL WE BECOME ANGELS WHEN WE DIE?

Many are comforted by the thought of their loved ones becoming angels upon death, especially if they were children. To entertain the idea that they have stepped into an angelic role brings peace to the unknown. However, this idea is not scripturally based.

As I mentioned earlier, the angels were all created at one time, and they do not have the ability to reproduce in the normal fashion (Matthew 22:30). There is also no scriptural evidence that the original number of these created beings will increase (Genesis 2:1–3).

One of my seminary colleagues said, "No sinner saved by grace would ever want to give up his exalted position in Christ by becoming an angel." There are no baby angels, period.

WHAT HAPPENS
TO THE BURIED BODY?

The buried physical body will remain on the earth awaiting Christ's return. Christ will raise the dead and reunite it with the soul (John 14:1–3). God has a specific time of His return, yet neither Jesus nor the angels are aware of that appointed time (Matthew 24:36–44).

According to 1 Thessalonians 4:16–17, "For the Lord himself [in person] will descend from heaven with a cry of command [war shout], with the voice of an archangel, and with the sound of the trumpet [summoning God's elect together for their glorification with Christ] of God. And the dead in Christ will rise first. Then we who are alive, who are left, will be caught up [raptured] together with them in the clouds to meet the Lord in the air, and so we will always be with the Lord."[21]

The term *rapture* means, "To carry off by force, snatch violently, suddenly."[22] As I studied this passage, I was moved

21 Robert Jamieson, A. R. Fausset, and David Brown, *Commentary Critical and Explanatory on the Whole Bible*. Logos Bible Scholar Software.

22 K. S. Wuest, *Wuest's Word Studies in the Greek New Testament*. Logos Bible Scholar Software.

by the sudden and violent snatching that will take place.
There is something so powerful about Jesus releasing a war
cry, awaking the dead, and then violently snatching them
from Satan's domain, the earth.

WILL WE RECOGNIZE EACH
OTHER IN HEAVEN?

I am confident that we will recognize each other in heaven.

According to the account of the disciples on the Mount
of Transfiguration, they witnessed Jesus speaking with Moses
and Elijah and they recognized each other. The disciples
had never met Moses and Elijah but immediately knew
who they were.

This gives tremendous hope for those who have walked
the path of abortion or miscarriage. That child has a body
according to Scripture, and from the account we just dis-
cussed, you will not only meet this precious child—you will
immediately "know" who they are, because we will be in the
era when we will know as we are known.[23]

Matthew tells us that when Jesus died, "The tombs also
were opened. And many bodies of the saints who had fallen
asleep were raised, and coming out of the tombs after his resurrection they went into the holy city and appeared to many"
(27:52–53). The fact that these people appeared to many

23 Jack Hayford, *I'll Hold You in Heaven*, 78.

suggests that they were recognizable and that people knew who they were.[24]

WHAT IS THE "SECOND DEATH"?

"Second death" refers to those who have chosen spiritual death, which is separation from God for eternity. It is important to understand that death is not the end for anyone. Regardless of the path that is chosen, eternity awaits in heaven with God or in the place of absolute hopelessness that the Bible refers to as hell.

It is the location where the spirit of the unbeliever will dwell. The Bible describes hell as "darkness, where there will be weeping and gnashing of teeth" (Matthew 8:12 NIV). According to 2 Thessalonians, its inhabitants will be "shut out from the presence of the Lord and from the glory of his might" (1:9 NIV).

The Scriptures never suggest that there will be a second opportunity to choose Christ after death. As a matter of fact, in Jesus' account of the rich man and Lazarus, no hope of crossing from hell into heaven is given.

The rich man in hell yelled out, "Father Abraham, have mercy on me, and send Lazarus to dip the end of his finger in water and cool my tongue, for I am in anguish in this flame."

Abraham replied to him, "Between us and you a great chasm has been fixed, in order that those who would pass

---

24 Wayne Grudem, *Sytematic Theology*, 835.

from here to you may not be able, and none may cross from there to us" (Luke 16:24–26).

This particular truth can be difficult to grasp. The thought of spending eternity suffering is a concept almost unbearable to fathom. Some would like to offer the doctrine of annihilationism as hope. This doctrine declares that unbelievers, either immediately upon death or else after suffering for a period of time, will simply cease to exist—God will annihilate them and they will no longer be.[25] However, there is simply no scriptural evidence to back this theory. God created us as eternal beings. Therefore, we will either live in heaven with Him for eternal life or will spend eternity in suffering (Matthew 25:46).

Unbelievers will pass into a state of eternal punishment immediately upon death; their bodies will not be raised until the day of final judgment. On that day, their bodies will be raised and reunited with their souls, and they will

Friends, it is so important that we not judge the state of another person's soul, as only God knows the hearts of His creation.

stand before God's throne for final judgment to be pronounced upon them in the body (Matthew 25:31–46; John 5:28–29; Acts 24:15; and Revelation 20:12–15).[26]

Friends, it is so important that we not judge the state of another person's soul, as only God knows the hearts of His creation. We are told in Psalm 96:13, "He will judge

---

25 Ibid., 823.

26 Ibid.

the world in righteousness, and the peoples in his faithfulness." Whatever takes place in the moments prior to taking
the last breath can only be known by that person and God
Himself.

Paul's response to the soul of the lost was "I have great
sorrow and unceasing anguish in my heart" (Romans 9:2).
This response should be ours as well, as God has placed His
attribute of love for others within our hearts for all of His
creation. The realization of hell for those that choose to deny
Christ should be the very thought that pushes us forward,
without fear, to share the gospel.

Also, we should not assume that those who claim to be
followers of Christ will all go to heaven. Matthew 7:21 says,
"Not everyone who says to me, 'Lord, Lord,' will enter the
kingdom of heaven, but the one who does the will of my
Father who is in heaven." Dr. Graham says this: "Don't fall
into Satan's trap by comparing yourself to anyone else. Set
your eyes instead on the One who died for you. Seek Him;
He will save you. Live for Him; He will open up Heaven's
doors for you."[27]

THE ULTIMATE DESTINATION
FOR BELIEVERS

According to the Book of Revelation, heaven is a "holy city,"

---

27 Billy Graham, *The Heaven Answer Book* (Nashville: Thomas Nelson, 2012), 148.

a place "prepared as a bride adorned for her husband" (21:2). "Death shall be no more, neither shall there be mourning, nor crying, nor pain" (21:4). We will drink "from the spring of the water of life without payment" (21:6). It has "the glory of God, its radiance like a most rare jewel, like a jasper, clear as crystal" (21:11). It is immense in size—we are not sure if this description is literal or symbolic, but it is massive— described as length measuring "12,000 stadia," or about 1,400 miles, and "its length and width and height are equal" (21:16). Parts of the city are described as being made of precious jewels of a variety of colors (21:18–21). It is free from all evil, for "nothing unclean will ever enter it, nor anyone who does what is detestable or false, but only those who are written in the Lamb's book of life" (21:27).

But how big is heaven in today's terms? Dr. Brown beautifully puts these details into earthly measures:

Heaven is laid out in perfect symmetry, covering 2,250,000 square miles with each side of the walled city roughly the same length as the distance from Seattle to the midpoint of Baja, California. In area it covers almost 65 percent of the continental United States.

From just inside each of the twelve gates of Heaven, the land begins an incredible ascent (at a 63-degree angle) for 750 miles until it peaks at the highest point, the mountain of God that extends 1,500 miles into the sky. That is more than 270 times higher than the 5.5-mile height of Mt. Everest. What an unbelievable view.[28]

As beautiful as this may sound, the mightiest truth is that we get to spend eternity in the presence of God Almighty. This is a lot to process, but I pray that it gives some idea of what the Scriptures affirm to believers as their eternal home. "He will dwell with them, and they will be his people, and God himself will be with them as their God. He will wipe away every tear from their eyes" (Revelation 21:3–4). There will be no more broken bodies, lives, or hearts. He promises.

This has been a most difficult chapter to tackle as some very sensitive issues have been addressed. The Scriptures declare that the "truth will set you free" (John 8:32). Although some of these might be painful to accept, I pray you will allow the Holy Spirit to comfort your heart and to bring more clarity and understanding where pain remains.

28 Daniel A. Brown, *What the Bible Reveals About Heaven* (Ventura: Regal, 1991), 199.

chapter nine

Mentoring, Orphanages, and Mercy

Mother's Day has been officially celebrated in America for more than one hundred years. When Anna Marie Jarvis's mother died on May 9, 1905, she wanted a way to honor her memory. The first Mother's Day service was held at her church two years after her mother's death. By 1914, the United States Congress had passed a law designating the second Sunday in May as Mother's Day.[29]

Mother's Day is a beautiful celebration of the women who raised us, encouraged us, and gave us life. It is also one of the most difficult holidays for women. I understand that it is supposed to be a day to be honored, but for many who have buried their mothers prematurely, have been abandoned by them, or simply have a relationship that is unhealthy, this specific day can bring much heartbreak. Then, there are

---

29 Jone Johnson Lewis, "Anna Jarvis and Mother's Day," *Womenshistory.About.com*, http://womenshistory.about.com/od/mothersday/a/anna_jarvis.htm.

those who desire to be mothers but have not yet conceived, and others who have buried children; this day magnifies their loss and disappointment. As you can imagine, it is a holiday most pastors dread for these reasons.

I was recently asked to speak at a Mother's Day service. I must admit I held the same reservations as many other pastors. How do you deliver a message to mothers when there are so many devastating circumstances within the congregation?

Whatever your circumstances, I pray this chapter brings further clarity and healing to your heart. This chapter is not just for women *or* mothers; rather it focuses on the call for each of us to live "in community" with one another—specifically, what does that mean, and how do we fulfill this directive?

THE MANY HATS OF A MOM

Each day as we pulled into our driveway, Ramsey would say, "Thank you, Jesus, for our beautiful house." This day was no different from the others. There was a love that would rise up each time I heard his little voice thanking God for blessing us with this home. His comment was so much more than a thankful heart to this mom; he was acknowledging our God. There is surely nothing sweeter than that to a mom's ears.

On May 25, the day before Ramsey's drowning, I took all three boys to a park in Cullman, Alabama. It was a sixty-five-acre natural area nestled in a five-hundred-foot canyon in the foothills of the Appalachian Mountains. There were hiking trails, picnic tables strewn throughout the park, bike trails, and rock climbing. They were all so excited! As for me, I was still unable to get around easily due to my progressing disease, but I was determined to have a great day with my boys.

I pulled into the park, and there was only one other car in the parking lot. I thought, *Well, that's odd.* Then I saw why—there was a huge rope hanging across the path with a sign dangling that read: Park Closed. So, we walked around the parking lot and were able to get close enough to just look over the side and into the canyon. That day I was the taxi driver, travel agent, and plan-B initiator.

As a child, one of my favorite games was playing dress up. You could put on a costume and become anyone in your mind that you wanted, then you could change your clothes. The sky was the limit. I remember using a hairbrush and slinging my long hair and instantly becoming Cher. Then I would line all my dolls in a row and become a teacher. I would use my arms to signal my bike as I would cross the road and instantly be driving a red convertible. I would do cartwheels across the front lawn, and boom . . . I was Olga Korbut of Russia, one of the greatest gymnasts of all time.

As young people we are taught that we can become anything we want to be. There are doctor's coats and stethoscopes, astronaut uniforms, princess dresses, pirate outfits, and even superhero costumes to encourage us. However, no one expects us to be all of those things at once. At least while we're kids.

As a mom, this becomes reality. We transition daily between the CEO of the home, scary monster under-the-bed checker, boo boo patrol, speech therapist, and janitor. The hats we get to wear are always changing. Emily Post says that removing your hat is a sign of respect and acknowledgement.[30] To all the moms, mothers, mums, mimis, and single dads fulfilling this role, I take off my hat to us all. It is hard work, and there are no prerequisites preparing us for stepping into the role.

I am reminded of several mothers who are introduced to us throughout the Scriptures:

> There was Eve, the mother of all the living
> (Genesis 3:20)
> Hagar, the mother of Ishmael (Genesis 16:1–4, 15)
> Sarah was the mother of Isaac (Genesis 18:10–14;
> 21:1–7)
> Rebekah was the mother of Esau and Jacob
> (Genesis 25:21–24; 27:5–17)
> Rachel was the mother of Joseph and Benjamin
> (Genesis 30:22–24; 35:16–20)
> Jochebed, mother of Aaron and Moses (Exodus
> 2:1–2; 6:20)
> Hannah was the mother to Samuel (1 Samuel
> 1:2–20)
> Bathsheba was the mother of Solomon (1 Kings
> 1:11)

---

30 Peggy Post, Anna Post, Lizzie Post, and Daniel Post Senning, *Emily Post's Etiquette: Manners for a New World* (New York: HarperCollins: 2011), 20.

Mary, the mother of Jesus (Luke 2:6–7; Matthew
1:18; Luke 1:26–38; 2:19)
Elizabeth was the mother of John the Baptist
(Luke 1:5–25, 57)

All these women were mothers by natural means—they
conceived and birthed children. They also wore many hats
and juggled daily, just as we do. No, they didn't always get
it right either.

Motherhood is also used throughout Scripture to illus-
trate the relationship between God and His people. "God's
care is like that of a mother bird," which is a common meta-
phor for His loving care. I believe that this is mirrored in the
gentleness and protection that is described in Psalm 91:1–6.

*He who dwells in the shelter of the Most High
will abide in the shadow of the Almighty.
I will say to the Lord, "My refuge and my fortress,
my God, in whom I trust."
For he will deliver you from the snare of the fowler
and from the deadly pestilence.
He will cover you with his pinions,
and under his wings you will find refuge;
his faithfulness is a shield and buckler.
You will not fear the terror of the night,
nor the arrow that flies by day,
nor the pestilence that stalks in darkness,
nor the destruction that wastes at noonday.*

There is such comfort when you can tuck away and almost feel hidden under His protection, under His wings. It's much like the feeling of being safe in a caregiver's arms as a child. I have spent much time in this place over the last several years, and there is no other rest to compare. Just as little ones climb into laps in search of security, we are basically in search of the same lap. As a woman who births a child holds the position of a mother, we hold a similar position in the heart of God. He nurtures us, protects us, and loves us, unconditionally.

There is such comfort when you can tuck away and almost feel hidden under His protection, under His wings.

When I think of a nursing infant, I immediately entertain the ideas of quiet, calmness, and dependency. The baby knows that protection and sufficiency are near. So gentle, so loving, and always on her mother's mind. A mother truly has the ability to release such depths of love and comfort into her children. Although some may have chosen to withhold these, God intended for them to be evident.

Sometimes we find this same nurturing in unexpected places.

THE TRUTH

When I was five years old, my mother was in the hospital having surgery, and her best friend took me to a healing service at a little country church. Back then I stuttered so badly that I was unable to ask for a peanut butter sandwich.

As a very shy child, I remember walking in the door of this unfamiliar church and seeing all the people staring back at me. There was a long wooden table in the front, and a man and several ladies stood around it. I walked in and the man told me to come forward. As I made my way to the front holding my caregiver's hand, my knees shook and my hands trembled.

The pastor picked me up and sat me on the table. I remember being terrified. He told me that they wanted to pray for me, and I wasn't sure what that meant. As they began to pray and pray and pray, I covered my ears and wept uncontrollably because I couldn't understand any of the words I was hearing. They were speaking in a foreign language that sounded like Russian to my little ears. I already knew I could not speak well, and now . . . I was sure I had lost my hearing!

The pastor said, "Ann, what would you like to say?"

I remember crying so hard and saying, "I don't know what to say!"

Just as the stuttering began, so did my healing happen—instantly. I never stuttered again.

MY SAFE PLACES

I was seven years old. She was a widow of eighty-two. She played the piano in the local Baptist church for over fifty years, and I had only attended church once—for the healing service.

Every afternoon after school I would get off the bus, drop my books at home, and cross the street to Mrs. Glasgow's house. It was the same thing every day: I would walk in and find a snack that she had prepared just for me.

Her home was my safe place. There was much physical and emotional abuse in my home; I believe my earlier stuttering was a result of this, as trauma oftentimes triggers stuttering. But Mrs. Glasgow was my light and my lifeline as a child.

Sitting there on that hard piano stool she would teach me about love, Jesus, relationships, finances, and life. From the first grade through my junior year in high school, she poured her wisdom over my life. She had no children, and I was the recipient of her spiritual inheritance.

Sitting there on that hard piano stool she would teach me about love, Jesus, relationships, finances, and life.

There was another important woman named Mrs. White. I remember the smell of her perfume and her shiny, red lips. Every Sunday, starting in the third grade, I would get off the church bus and run into the sanctuary so I could sit with her. Although my family didn't go to church, I was allowed to go since the church bus picked me up and dropped me off. I am sure she knew that I was the little girl who rode the church bus each week, alone.

Each Sunday we sat in the service, chewing gum together, with her arm around my little shoulders. She surrounded me with safety! Even though she had a daughter, she always made sure there was room for me.

The Lord placed these women in my life to show me the way and to show me how to love like Him. They planted seeds in my heart about His Word.

Mrs. Glasgow loved me as though I was her own, and she taught me invaluable life lessons. I watched Mrs. White love her husband and her daughter. I listened to how she spoke so tenderly to them. God was aligning my life before I even said "Yes" to Him. He was protecting my little heart and orchestrating my life at such a young age. These two spiritual moms altered my path!

WHAT MAKES A MOM?

So, what (and who) exactly is a mother? Dictionary.com defines *mother* as: "a female parent or a woman having the status, function, or authority of a female parent" or someone who tends, nurses, or raises. From this definition I believe a mother is not necessarily someone who gives natural birth to a child. We are told that a mother tends to or takes care of someone else. A mother raises a child. The definition states that it is a person holding the status or walking in the function. This is a very important truth. Ladies, whether you have physically birthed a child, adopted a child, have children through a blended household, or have spiritual children, you have the ability to nurture life.

As a result of Ramsey's drowning, I've realized that I have a need to mother and nurture even more. Perhaps this loss gave me a broader understanding of mothering and a clearer view of those available opportunities.

I have birthed three sons, but I have over forty spiritual sons and daughters. I had not planned to have spiritual sons and daughters, yet suddenly, I realized I was pouring into young people's lives just as Mrs. White and Mrs. Glasgow had mine. The youngest of my spiritual children just turned eighteen months old. He is too young to understand doctrinal truths so I approach his need differently. I often hold him during worship, and as I hold him in my arms, he puts his tiny little hand in mine as mine are raised to the Lord. He may not understand theological truths, but I am teaching him that we lift our hands to a holy God.

Being a spiritual mom is limited by neither age nor denomination. I have a spiritual daughter that is eighty-four years old. She gave her life to the Lord at age seventy-six. She has really bad shoulders, and she called me a couple of weeks ago to say that during worship she took her "good" arm and helped hold up her "bad" arm so she could lift her hands in worship. She attends a very conservative church and said, "I was the only one with my hand lifted, but what are they going to do? Try to stop an eighty-four-year-old widow from worshipping?" This spiritual daughter . . . is my mom!

POURING INTO OTHERS

My husband and I were recently discussing how so many athletes are drafted out of high school and lack the skill set and maturity to survive an adult atmosphere. We often hear how these young men and favored athletes make poor choices and oftentimes find themselves in jail. More times than not, these young men come from broken homes with little or no authority figures in their lives. They have no one holding them accountable for their actions, and when the opportunity knocks, they plow through the door and then flounder because of their lack of direction.

The Apostle Paul told the church in Corinth that he was their spiritual father and that he would help them become the people God intended. He would be their life coach. He would teach, correct, nudge, and love them into the place God purposed. Just as those athletes need accountability, we do as well. Some of us have natural parents that held us accountable, and some of us have spiritual parents. God intended for us to live "in community" and to "do" life together.

There are many powerful examples of spiritual parenting strewn throughout the Scriptures, but this one is a favorite. Her name was Naomi. Her husband, Elimelech, died, and she was left with her two sons. They married Moabite women, Orpah and Ruth. Within ten years, Naomi's sons also died. When Ruth's husband died, she begged to stay with her mother-in-law, Naomi. Naomi said to her daughters-in-law: "Go, return each of you to her mother's house."

They replied, "No, we will return with you to your people." Naomi tried again to send them home to start a new life, to find new husbands. She thought she had nothing to give them (Ruth 1:1–13).

Orpah kissed her mother-in-law and headed back to Moab. Ruth made a different decision: "Do not urge me to leave you . . . Where you go I will go, and where you lodge I will lodge. Your people shall be my people, and your God my God. Where you die I will die, and there will I be buried" (1:16–17).

For years I struggled with Ruth's decision to stay with Naomi. There was nothing there for her. She was a foreigner in Naomi's land. What was it that caused her to beg to stay with her mother-in-law?

Suddenly, Naomi was back in the nurturing business. Her broken heart after burying a husband and two sons began to heal as she taught Ruth how to care for a household, and as she showed her how to respond to hardship and even tragedy. Naomi had flaws in her mindset concerning God and His part in her devastation—all the while she was teaching Ruth to hold on, giving her hope where she previously had none. When God gave Ruth a new husband, though she was a foreigner in the land, she was able to meet the challenges of the culture because of the teachings of Naomi. Because she said "Yes" to mentoring this young woman, she became part of the genealogy of Jesus Christ as the great-grandmother of King David.

Then there was a man named Barnabas. Most people

called him "the encourager." He had an inspiring influence (Acts 11:23–26). He spoke life—encouraging and empowering everyone he came in contact with. I want people to walk away from me feeling better than when we met. I recently read this quote: "People will not remember what you said; only how you made them feel." Barnabas was a spiritual parent to many.

He mentored the Apostle Paul. He mentored John Mark (Acts 12–13). If you recall the story, John went on the first missionary journey of Barnabas, and failed miserably. He quit and went back home to Jerusalem. It is so important to understand that the mentor never gave up and John Mark did not finish as a failure. Although we are sowing into people who may fail, we must choose to come alongside them and help them walk, step-by-step, if necessary.

The character and nature of God will be more evident in how we walk, talk, love, and reach out to one another.

To be an encourager like Barnabas requires doing what he did. He used his spiritual gifts, his love of Jesus as well as people, to empower others. In order to be an encourager we need a ministry to ourselves, first. We have to align ourselves with what God is doing. It is impossible to encourage others if we are not properly encouraged.

There is just something very empowering about spending time in the presence of God. Suddenly, you realize you are speaking life into others. The character and nature of God will be more evident in how we walk, talk, love, and reach out to one another. The closer we are discipling with Him, the more our life should look like it! We will not be carrying a sign and screaming at the young woman on the corner; we will be reaching out with a blanket and the compassion of God for her. Regardless of where your pain may be taking you, choose to speak life into one another's circumstances. You will see that the encouragement will encourage you as well.

I remember several difficult times in my life when I suffered as a result of my own poor choices. I did not need someone to point out my shortcomings because I clearly understood those. I just needed someone to help me believe again. I had lost hope and needed some encouragement. The truth is that we all need encouragement, whether we are currently suffering or not. Just because we are not struggling today does not mean we will not tomorrow. Remember to speak life at every opportunity.

ROLE MODELS

One of the greatest role models of spiritual parenting, mentoring, and discipleship-making is that of Jesus. He took twelve men from various walks of life and discipled them by "doing life": teaching, praying, and encouraging them. They became the foundation of the Church. They were a bunch of misfits whom Jesus chose. They were doubters; they refused to forgive; they were jealous; and they basically lacked faith. Jesus never focused on these shortcomings, but rather on how to empower them to fulfill their mission. They became great examples of what investment into someone else can produce.

Then there was Timothy. "Timothy, who would you give credit for helping shape your life?" He responds, "Oh, my grandmother Lois, my mother Eunice, and the Apostle Paul." I believe he would follow with this:

I also spent some time with Luke, John Mark, Barnabas, Silas, and Titus, but it was Paul who mentored me in the faith and in leadership. He was truly my greatest fan. I was not a very strong leader, and honestly, I was quite fearful of what others thought of me. I guess most would describe me as timid. It really did hinder me while I was preaching, but Paul was constantly instructing me and encouraging me to be bold and deliver the Word with authority. Remember when I made a mess at the church in Corinth? Paul used it as a teaching moment. He came alongside me and went back with me to Corinth. He never gave up on me. He showed me how to step up and win.

I am encouraged by all these examples of spiritual fathers freely giving their lives to others. God created the woman to be the nurturer but I am overwhelmed by the ability of these men to nurture. Let us learn from this. Nurturing another's life does not require holding a "biological" position in their life; rather, it has everything to do with your heart.

THE PROMISE

There was a woman named Jochebed who bore a son during the time when Pharaoh had ordered that all male, Hebrew infants be put to death (Exodus 1:15–22). She took a basket, which was her only method of protecting the baby from the crocodiles; she waterproofed it, and sent the baby down the river. The baby's sister, Miriam, watched from afar as Pharaoh's daughter spotted the basket and retrieved the child. She eventually adopted little Moses into the royal family.

A young girl, Esther, was adopted by her cousins after her parents' death. She became queen and God used her to bring deliverance to the Jews. I am also reminded of Jesus' conception. He was conceived through the Holy Spirit rather than through the seed of man (Matthew 1:18). He was adopted, in a sense, and raised by His mother's husband, Joseph.

Whenever we make the decision to give our hearts and our lives to Christ, we become part of a new family, His family.

Whenever we make the decision to give our hearts and our lives to Christ, we become part of a new family, His family. This new position is not through natural means of a rebirth as Nicodemus questioned in the Book of John, but rather it is through adoption. Romans 8:15 declares, "For you did not receive the spirit of slavery to fall back into fear, but you have received the Spirit of adoption as sons, by whom we cry, 'Abba! Father!'" "Theologically, the act of God by which believers become

members of 'God's family' with all the privileges and obliga-
tions of family membership" is referred to as *adoption*.[31]

When I consider the act of adoption I immediately think
of how adoption is based on love and choice. I believe that
choosing to give yourself away and into another person's life
is very much the same sentiment as adoption. It is a choice,
and it is made in love.

In order to live in community and to "do life" together,
we must choose to be intentional in contributing to others'
lives. As a result of the Fall, we are much more likely to
isolate ourselves rather than open up to someone else. I am
so thankful that God placed two god-fearing women in
my life to help shape my path. They each chose selflessness
and entered into this little girl's life. When I received the call
to seminary, I was reminded of the groundwork they both
laid out for me. They loved the Word of God, worship, and
Jesus! This was the "seed" that had been placed in my soul
and lay dormant until the proper time.

WALKING A NEW PATH

After several years of seminary and a Master of Divinity
degree, I was given the opportunity to nurture others' paths as
well as their souls. As a teacher, I would spend hours teaching
Bible courses to college students and Bible classes offered to

31 Walter A. Elwell and Barry J. Beitzel, *Baker Encyclopedia of the Bible* (Grand Rapids:
Baker, 1988).

the church. As a pastor, I realized that a tremendous part of the position is not only equipping but coaching others toward their call. And as an international conference speaker, I have the opportunity to empower men and women and help lay foundations for life. Not only does God give me the opportunity to do these things corporately, but I "get" to resource upcoming leaders as well as those on foreign soil to fulfill their dreams.

All of this, because I was in search of healing for my broken heart, wholeness for my mind because of depression, and understanding for the reason that such a tragedy could happen to "good" Christian people. Sometimes it feels as though I am an extension of what two elderly women started within me. I'm carrying their flame forward to new generations.

I didn't know that May 26, 2000, was the last day I would get to "mommy" Ramsey. I didn't know that I would not have an opportunity to get a do-over on May 27, in case I needed it. Friends, every day should be lived as if it's the last. I know— it's a little cliché. But the truth is we really may not get the opportunity to say we are sorry or "Son, I missed it."

I wasn't ready then and I am still not ready to stop mothering. As long as I still have life in my body, I will continue pouring into others. I have learned much over the years about being a mom and a wife. I am taking that knowledge and moving forward to the next phase.

There are many, many children across the world who need someone to step in and say "Yes." We need mothers. We need fathers. We need concerned neighbors and friends who will go the extra mile when they see someone in need. Whether you teach Sunday school, mentor another, support a child or a family through a nonprofit, or simply look for opportunities to volunteer in your city—your time and encouragement are needed and appreciated. It doesn't cost you much and it pays endless dividends.

There are many, many children across the world who need someone to step in and say "Yes." We need mothers. We need fathers.

Right now, there are 132 million orphaned children in the world needing you to say "Yes."[32] The opportunity is before you. The children are calling you! Ramsey's Rescue, a children's home in Ramsey's honor, is just on the horizon. So, c'mon, let's go!

Please, won't you join me in this next step?

---

32 "Orphans—Press Centre," *Unicef,* last modified August 21, 2008, http://www.unicef.org/media/media_45279.html.

chapter ten

Waite Minus One

My son, Chandler, at the age of twenty, spent a year studying abroad in Thailand and Austria during his sophomore
year of college. He called from Austria one morning and
began a conversation about his experiences of the day. As we
continued our talk, he shared with me that since Ramsey's
passing, he really did not like to be alone. He explained that
his desire was to stay busy and to surround himself with
friends. When he described his childhood as being "cradled
in death," I was shocked. *What? Cradled in death?*

But to him, it made sense. He recalls Ramsey's passing
as being a real wakeup call. Experiencing death that closely
caused him to realize the "suddenly" of God. The fear of
the Lord gripped him at a very early age. This fear that
Chandler mentioned to me was the very same fear of the
Lord that I experienced during that tragedy. I realized that
"He holds my very last breath in his hand" should be taken
literally. We are not promised a specific length of time on

this earth, and that truth became real to our family. We've never taken our time for granted since.

For the Waite family, time is a gift we don't feel we deserve, and it can be taken from us at any moment. We love hard, we love deep, and we strive every day to live without any regret. I believe the reality of the unknown time that we each have has caused our family to love each other like we could not have, had we not experienced Ramsey's drowning.

COURAGE UNDER FIRE

My sons have a very strong relationship with each other. We are not promised a moment in time, and I believe those two boys looking at Ramsey in my arms in the consultation room after his passing was a moment of reality they will never forget. I believe this is the reason they have the mindset that they *will* change the world. They often tell me that they believe they have more to prove because of Ramsey's passing. You know, since he didn't get to do life. He didn't get to make a contribution to society. So we all share a common bond and hope in healing, daily.

I remember the day Chandler met with the American Ambassador to Austria. He was having a class the following day in the OPEC building in Vienna. He'd become a real world traveler, and his schedule was filled with the most exciting and life-changing opportunities for the upcoming weeks!

As he gave me details of all his appointments, he also

commented that although the opportunities were of great magnitude, he oftentimes finds himself at the end of the day feeling like, "Is that all that this day holds?" Wow! He is always looking for the next thing. It is not an ungrateful heart, but rather one that wants all that God would trust him with. So, this feeling of a childhood being cradled in death has actually birthed a very courageous spirit within him.

He does not have fear of taking the giant leap forward, but instead the fear of missing an opportunity is far more of a crippling idea. Perhaps the understanding of how close death is at all times is the very truth that catapults him forward, removing all the thoughts of "What if I fail?" from his psyche.

This courageous spirit surrounds my oldest son Benjamin as well. After completing his college degree on a baseball scholarship, he landed in Germany to continue playing ball. After establishing himself professionally in Europe—Germany, Switzerland, Czech Republic, Austria, Bulgaria, and two seasons in South Africa—he decided to step out of his comfort zone and take the big leap. He could have continued in the luxury of worldwide travel woven into playing professional ball. He had already made it. However, his mindset is that it is far better to fall flat on your face in an attempt to pursue it all than it is to spend a lifetime wondering "What if?"'

His eyes are currently set on pursuing a position in the MLB. He moved back to the United States and began to play. He's played in Colorado, New Mexico, Kansas, and Texas. He continues to train and play abroad during the off-season in preparation for the next stateside opportunity.

I believe only God could have placed the passion he has for this goal inside of him. He consistently pushes through the barriers that attempt to distract, including two reconstructive shoulder surgeries. He pitches harder and is more effective post surgery, which is nothing shy of a miracle. He is driven. He is successful. He is courageous.

My husband has the same drive to succeed and take chances in the face of complacency. He describes it this way:

It is a wall you hit, suddenly; you hurt from the impact and you cannot go forward anymore. You will ultimately change directions. The wall is permanent and blocks you from even seeing where you were headed. You will stand at the wall rubbing your injuries (significant) awhile, probably a couple of years. I sat at that wall suffering, looking up to G_d, worshipping and praying with a totally new understanding of Him. He is who I knew Him to be, but He had shown Himself in a real omnipotent, life, death, give, and take, my word is not the last word, its the only-word way.

I am different, I see different, I relate different, I pray different, I react different, I expect different. G_d is consequential in a way I did not understand prior to Ramsey's drowning.

After a while you get up and check out the other 180 degrees of direction that are left to you. You take a step away from the wall, because you have been there long enough to realize its permanence. I recommend you pick up what is good of what you have left, leave what is worthless (new values reside in you now), and move in a direction that makes sense practically and spiritually.

We have all been changed by this journey. It was not one we ever expected to face; but it has changed us into a family of four that lives without regret, walks in great confidence knowing who we are "in Him," and is always willing to obey Him, no matter what it looks like.

Trust Him to show up when you think you cannot take another hit, and most importantly, know that nothing happens in your life that He is unaware of.

Life is too short to walk in fear, which ultimately paralyzes and keeps you from being effective. It is too short to walk in unforgiveness. Love with your whole heart. Forgive when it is the most difficult. Trust Him to show up when you think you cannot take another hit, and most importantly, know that nothing happens in your life that He is unaware of.

Remember, friends, He loves you like no one else can! He is forever faithful and He is near, no matter where your journey takes you.

Forever His,
Angelia

about the author

Angelia Waite is a unique theologian. She has been captured by the Lord Jesus Christ and her life experiences have shaped and amplified her representation of the Holy Spirit. She is enthusiastic, entertaining, visional, courageous, and original.

She is a graduate of The King's University in Van Nuys, California, holding a Master of Divinity. She is successful in her personal ministry, Angelia Waite Ministries, Inc. She is also a licensed associate pastor at her local church, Restoration Foursquare Church in Madison, Alabama, and ordained through R3 Alliance, Inc. Huntsville, Alabama. She is the founder and chairman of Ramsey's Rescue, Inc.

Experienced in missions and conference work, Angelia is a gifted communicator and is effective in a variety of venues.

She is married to Dr. Jay Waite, a practicing veterinarian in Madison, Alabama. They have been married for more than thirty years and they have three sons: Benji, Chandler, and Ramsey.

FOR THE LATEST UPDATES ON
RAMSEY'S RESCUE, PLEASE VISIT:

www.RamseysRescue.org

FOR THE LATEST IN NEWS AND MINISTRY
INFORMATION, PLEASE VISIT:

www.AngeliaWaite.org
www.Facebook.com/AngeliaWaite
www.Twitter.com/AngeliaWaite
Instagram: @angeliawaiteministries
YouTube: Angelia Waite Ministries

FOR BOOKING ENGAGEMENTS,
PLEASE CONTACT OUR OFFICE:

Angelia Waite Ministries
P. O. Box 238
Madison, AL 35758
Office Phone: 256-683-5511
Email: info@angeliawaite.org